# MEALS ON KEELS

New Grimsby Sound with Cromwell's Castle on Tresco (left) and Hangman's Rock, over the bow, on Bryher, Isles of Scilly

Front Cover:
Terns in the Skerries lagoon off Carmel Head, north west Anglesey
Back Cover :
Pebbles on Newborough beach, Anglesey

Copyright © 2020 by Rosa Mari Edlin Williams

All rights reserved. No part of this book may be reproduced, transmitted or distributed in any form or by any electronic or mechanical means, including information storage and retrieval systems, without permission in writing from the copyright owner except for the use of brief quotations in a book review.

FIRST PAPERBACK EDITION OCTOBER 2020
ISBN 979-8-6768-7284-7 (paperback)
Published by Amazon Publishing

ROSA MARI EDLIN WILLIAMS

# MEALS ON KEELS

A personal culinary journey afloat

COOKING IN CONFINED SPACES WITH LIMITED EQUIPMENT

On board a yacht, powerboat, caravan, mobile home, campervan, tent, a self catering holiday cottage or small bedsit, in fact for anyone who wants to cook whether at home or on their next adventure

Low water, Old Grimsby, Tresco, Isles of Scilly

Llandwyn Island at low tide looking towards Snowdonia

A quick swim at beautiful Saye beach, Alderney, after crossing the Channel.

## Dedication

To my husband David, a superb yachtsman, who has inspired and encouraged the writing of this book and who has travelled some of this journey with me on the water as well as through life.

I also wish to thank all the students who have cooked and tested the recipes when studying RYA courses on board and their encouragement to produce a cookbook.

South Stack Lighthouse, Anglesey

Regularly visited beautiful Porthdinllaen on the Llŷn Peninsular

# Contents

| | Page |
|---|---|
| Introduction | 7 |
| Cooking in Confined Spaces | 9 |
| Provisioning | 11 |
| Essential Cooking Equipment | 15 |
| Breakfast | 21 |
| Lunch | 41 |
| Salads and Vegetables | 63 |
| RYA Training Course Meals | 77 |
| Dinner | 93 |
| Laying up Leftovers | 125 |
| Desserts | 135 |
| Baking | 147 |
| Index | 168 |
| Recipe Index | 173 |
| The Author | 175 |
| Acknowledgements | 177 |

Crinan Basin, Sound of Jura, before heading down the canal

# MEALS ON KEELS

This book is inspired by the places travelled while under sail, dishes prepared on board or eaten in the locality embodying a sense of place. It has also been encouraged by the many aspiring sailors who have passed through our RYA training centre on Anglesey and charterers.  It is a sailing life journey which started in Australia and continued in Malaysia, Wales, the Mediterranean, the Scilly Isles and Cornwall, The Channel Islands, Scotland, Northern Ireland and France.  The journey has not yet ended but this is the start of a culinary adventure on a keel.  Each region visited has its own special magic which comes out in the food.

Setting up an RYA training centre meant we had to ensure students could provision a yacht and prepare the food that had been provided.  We all know the importance of a delicious hot meal after a long day afloat sometimes in challenging conditions.   A dish well-cooked is essential for morale and keeps everyone on board happy and well and sitting around the saloon table sharing food with likeminded students fosters and forges new lasting friendships.  Some of  these recipes have been prepared by students over the years and requested on many occasions,  so are included as promised.

As a Cordon Bleu cook, preparing meals in a small restricted place with few utensils and limited cooking facilities, has never been a barrier to eating well prepared, delicious food.  The recipes are tested in confined spaces and some have been cooked by our aspiring competent crews,  day skippers, coastal skippers and yacht masters, keen to learn how to live well on board.

However, this book is for anyone who wants to cook delicious, nutritious meals whether at home or on their next adventure under sail or on land.

Freshly baked wholemeal loaf cooling in the galley on board

# COOKING IN CONFINED SPACES WITH LIMITED FACILITIES AND EQUIPMENT

On board a yacht, powerboat, caravan, mobile home, campervan, tent, a self-catering holiday cottage or small bedsit, in fact for anyone who wants to cook whether at home or on their next adventure

A galley (or kitchen) on a yacht, power boat, caravan, mobile home, camper van or in a bed sit is confined so meal planning and preparation is essential in such small spaces with limited equipment. With careful thought it is possible to prepare nutritious, appetising meals without resorting to ready-made meals or food that does not provide good nourishment. Next to voyage planning meal planning is of vital importance when sailing. It should never be an after thought and a well designed menu with all the necessary ingredients is vital for a successful journey on the water and through life.

A boat will usually have a small gas oven with two rings, one fridge or top loading cool box and a sink. It also has limited cupboard space for saucepans and cooking utensils and needs to be well planned and organised to make cooking in any weather as easy as possible, as well as enabling you to tie yourself on when cooking in bad conditions.

Whether underway or moored, plan the meal around two pot cooking such as a chilli and rice with guacamole, grated cheese and corn chips. Always tidy up as you go along as there is no room for piles of dirty dishes which can cause a hazard and it keeps washing up to a minimum at the end of the meal. Keeping the work space tidy means lockers and the top loading cool box are accessible with no danger of accidents from food spills. Take all ingredients and cooking pots you need out of lockers and cool box so you are not constantly having to clear the work surface to get at them.

Fresh fish and homemade produce. New Grimsby, Isles of Scilly

# Provisioning

When provisioning it is essential to plan meals for the duration of your voyage, whether a long weekend, several days or weeks.  Decide what you will cook and choose the required ingredients.  Not all the items listed are necessary and these only act as a guide for a well stocked cupboard.  Provisioning is not an exact science and when travelling to other countries and regions it isn't always possible to find the items listed in the recipes.  I have tried to keep the list of ingredients short but to still prepare delicious food.  Improvisation is part of the adventure so tackle it with ingenuity.

# Provisioning

The provisions are dependant on personal preference so these pages act as a guide. If conditions are difficult cooking a meal with food that is easily prepared is essential. It is important to keep strength and morale up with nourishing food.

## Dried food

Wholemeal rice
Basmati rice
Couscous
Textured soya protein chunks
Textured soya protein mince
Pasta
Biscuits such as digestives, rich tea or ginger
Wholemeal flour
Dried yeast
Mixed nuts
Porridge oats
Dried apricots
Prunes
Sultanas or raisins
Flaked nuts
Chopped hazelnuts
Walnuts
Cereals such as apricot wheats, Weetabix, Shredded Wheat
Red lentils, puy lentils
Ground almonds
Dried fruit salad
Tea
Coffee
Sugar and muscovado or molasses sugar
Herbal teas
Ryvita or other savoury crackers
Seed mix
Granola
Pine nuts

## Tinned food, food in jars and prepared food

Beans in water such as cannellini beans, chick peas and lentils
Baked beans
Tinned sweetcorn
Tinned tuna and other tinned fish
Pesto
Sundried tomatoes
Tinned chopped tomatoes
Olives
Marmalade and jam
Marmite
Tomato puree in a tube
Olive oil
Vinegar
Pesto
Tinned soup
Tinned fruit in fruit juice
Ready made custard
Fruit pies
Cakes
Cordials
Almond milk
Peanut butter
Dijon mustard
Soy sauce
Chilli sauce
Spanish chicken sauce
Red wine sauce
Balti curry sauce
Mango chutney

# Provisioning

Only buy enough fresh ingredients to last up to 5 days.  If you have limited refrigeration only buy what can be kept safely and look for preserved alternatives if possible.

## Fresh food
Eggs (they can last longer than 5 days)
Meat
Halloumi
Mozzarella
Cheddar
Sliced Ham
Vegetarian sausages
Vegetarian burgers
Salad vegetables
Butternut squash
Broccoli
Potatoes
Onions
Garlic
Mushrooms
Avocado
Kale
Lemons
Spinach
Feta
Aubergines
Courgettes
Carrots
Peppers
Celery
Fresh Fruit
Butter
Bread
Naan bread
Fresh ginger
Tofu
Yoghurt
Butternut squash
Fresh fish

## Herbs, spices and flavourings
Ground turmeric
Ground Cumin
Ground Cinnamon
Ground ginger
Curry Powder
Bay leaves
Dried oregano
Dried mixed herbs
Dried basil
Ground pepper
Cinnamon sticks
Sea salt
Bouillon
Stockpots
Mustard
Star anise
Dried chillies
Dried parsley
Dried rosemary
Dried thyme
Ground allspice
Ground coriander
Ground mixed spices

Breakfast in the cockpit Old Grimsby, Tresco, Isles of Scilly

# Essential Cooking Equipment

Each galley will have its own limited locker space and configuration but we will all agree that space is at a premium so choosing appropriate cooking utensils is essential. Keeping weight down to a minimum is also important so choose the lightest, most suitable items you can find. I have listed the items I use in my galley and have nothing surplus that never or rarely gets used. Always choose stainless steel for metal objects as sea air is corrosive and will degrade non stainless items. If you can avoid it don't choose glass unless it can be carefully and safely stowed. There are several attractive alternatives that are much safer such as melamine or enamel ware.

# A Well Equipped Galley

- Choose 3 saucepans, a large, medium and small and if possible with short handles such as those illustrated for safety.
- A pressure cooker to halve cooking time if needed. I have chosen a Tefal Clipso Minut Perfect.
- A non stick deep frying pan as large as possible to fit on the gas stove allowing room for another pan beside it and if possible large enough to stir fry vegetables. A pan with a removable handle makes storage easier.
- 2 Simmermat stovetop heat diffusers
- 2 non-stick baking sheets
- 2 wooden chopping boards. Wooden boards can be used for hot items or for serving food , not just for chopping ingredients.
- A folding vegetable steamer basket
- 1 loaf tin
- A measuring jug that will also provide cup measurements.
- A set of measuring spoons
- Nesting mixing bowls although I use salad and eating bowls on board
- 1 non stick muffin/cupcake tin or silicone for 12 muffins or individual silicone baking cups
- 1 roasting tin
- Wine glasses, melamine or glass if can be stowed safely (see top right)
- Tumblers, melamine
- Stackable melamine mugs
- Bowls, melamine or enamelled steel
- Dinner plates, melamine or enamelled steel
- Colander
- Egg cups

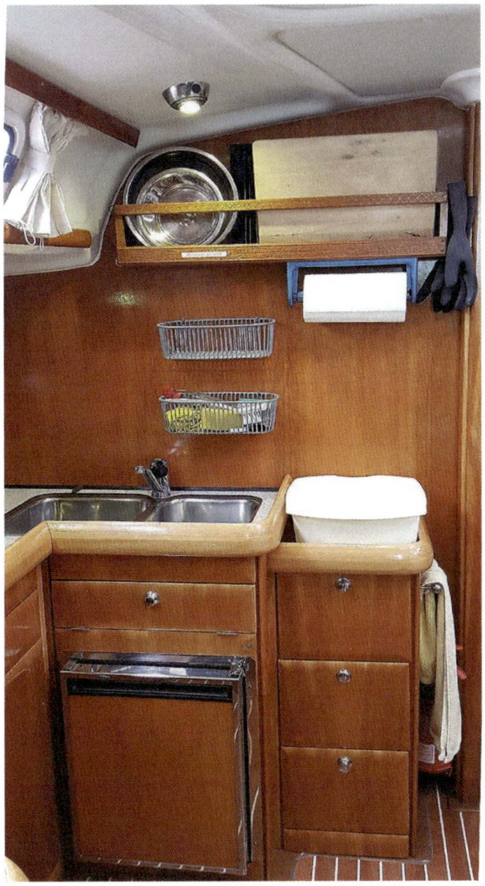

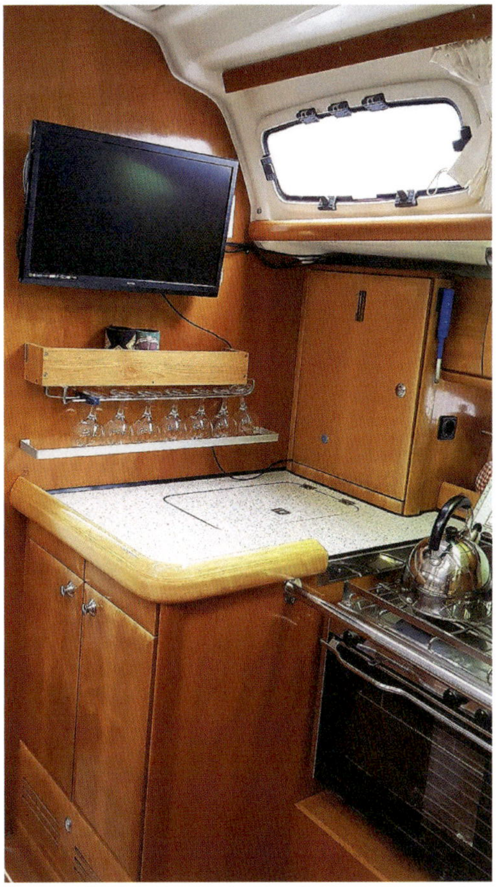

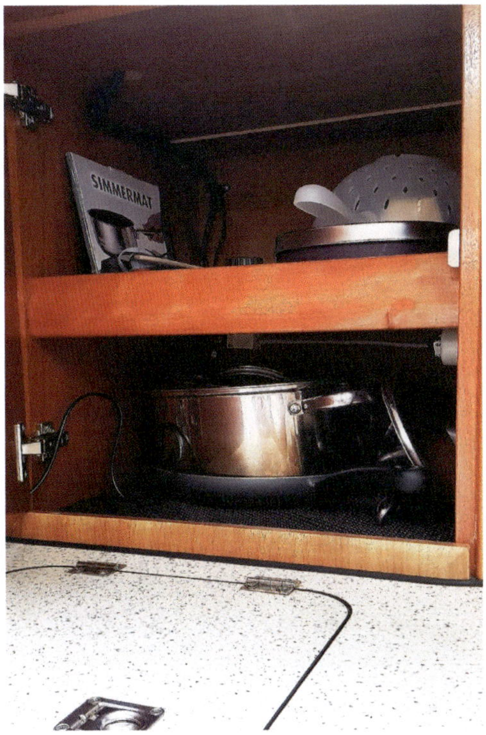
SIMMERMAT

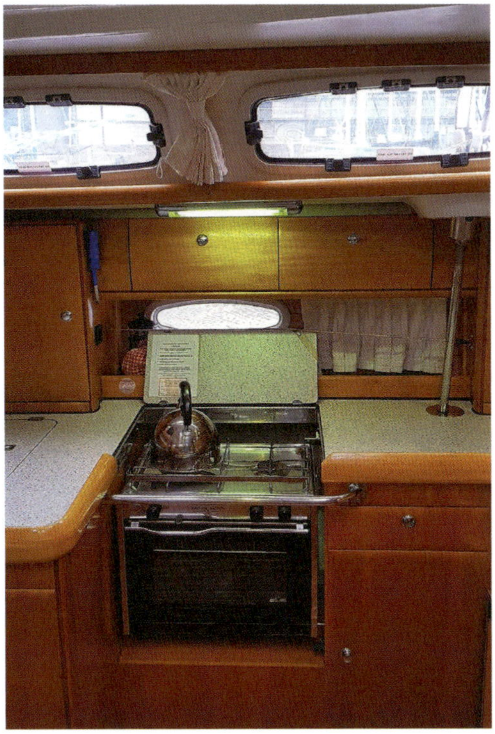

# A Well Equipped Galley

- A casserole dish 24 cm approximately that can double up as a quiche/pie dish
- 4 slice camping gas toaster
- Compact digital weighing scales
- Insulated mugs
- Large bowls for eating when underway
- 2 large serving spoons, one slotted
- Kitchen scissors
- Containers with lids for storing dried food and leftovers. Square or rectangular are stackable and maximise locker and fridge space.
- Lemon Squeezer
- Vegetable peeler
- Garlic press
- Soup ladle
- Wooden spoons
- Silicone lids
- Spatula
- Non stick or silicone fish slice
- Rotary or hand held whisk
- Screw top jars, 350—500 ml
- Cake tin, 17cm
- Potato masher
- Oven gloves

19

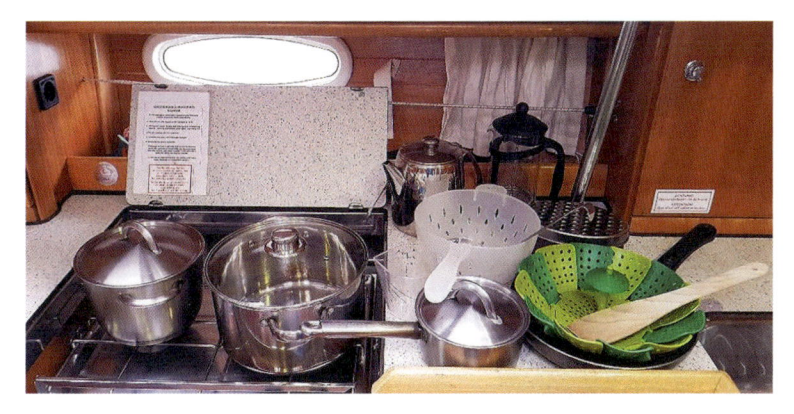

The sparrows joined us for tea in the Abbey Garden, Tresco, Isles of Scilly

# Breakfast

Such an important start to the day wherever you are and can be prepared whilst underway if you have an early tide to catch and calm conditions. It must be nutritious and easy to assemble. If casting off before breakfast ensure that any crew member who may suffer from seasickness has a cup of tea and a ships biscuit or two before departure.

From a safety and cleaning perspective I don't cook a fried breakfast on board but have included a variation which may satisfy those who enjoy a hot breakfast. I think this should be reserved for mornings tied up to a pontoon or at anchor. If you can step ashore go in search of the best cooked breakfast which is so anticipated and one of the simple pleasures after a long hard sail. Other hot alternatives are included that can be prepared in safety and with minimal mess.

East Loch Tarbert, Argyll

# Spiced Porridge

*Serves 2*

I first tried this porridge whilst on a yoga retreat in North Wales. It can be adapted to personal taste using spices you may have in your store cupboard on board. The ingredients are a matter of personal taste so experiment to find your perfect porridge. Make the porridge the consistency you prefer by adding more or less liquid. This recipe is enough for two so just double up on the ingredients if preparing it for a larger group.

*1 cup of wholemeal rolled oats*

*1 ½ cups of almond milk*

*1 cup water*

*½ teaspoon ground cinnamon*

*¼ teaspoon ground cumin*

*½ teaspoon ground turmeric*

*A little ground pepper*

*½ cup sultanas*

Mix all the ingredients together in a saucepan and put on a low heat. Bring to the boil, stirring all the time. so that the mixture does not stick to the bottom of the pan and burn. When the porridge has come to the boil just simmer very gently still stirring until it has thickened. Spoon into two bowls and serve. I serve it topped with molasses or honey, flaked almonds, sunflower seeds, pumpkin seeds, toasted chopped hazelnuts, walnuts, natural yogurt and a large bowl of fruit salad.

**Alternative or additional flavours**: Add lemon, lime or orange zest, dried apricots, chopped dates, chopped prunes, mixed nuts

23

# Cooked Breakfast

Cooking an English breakfast on board can create a large quantity of washing up and a cleaning challenge. Grease spatter and fat that needs disposing of should be avoided. This is a cooking method that provides all the pleasure with less mess.

## Gammon Steaks with Fried Egg, Mushrooms and Beans

Serves 1

*½ - 1 gammon steak per person or 2—3 vegetarian sausages or burgers (mozzarella) per person*

*1 – 2 eggs per person*

*½ tin of baked beans per person*

*A handful of mushrooms per person*

*Olive oil*

*Toast or wholemeal bread*

Place each gammon steak or sausages on a piece of foil, close the foil and place the package on a baking tray and put in a moderately hot oven 200°C, 180°C fan, Gas 6, for 10—15 minutes or until sizzling. Open the foil a little to allow the gammon to brown. Put the baked beans in a saucepan and heat, stirring occasionally. Meanwhile heat a little oil in a non-stick frying pan and add the mushrooms, cover with lid to avoid spatter and cook over medium heat until browned. Keep the mushrooms warm on some foil in the oven. Heat a little oil in the frying pan and start to fry the eggs. Make the toast and stack on a plate. Serve the gammon, mushrooms, baked beans and lastly the fried egg with the toast stack or bread.

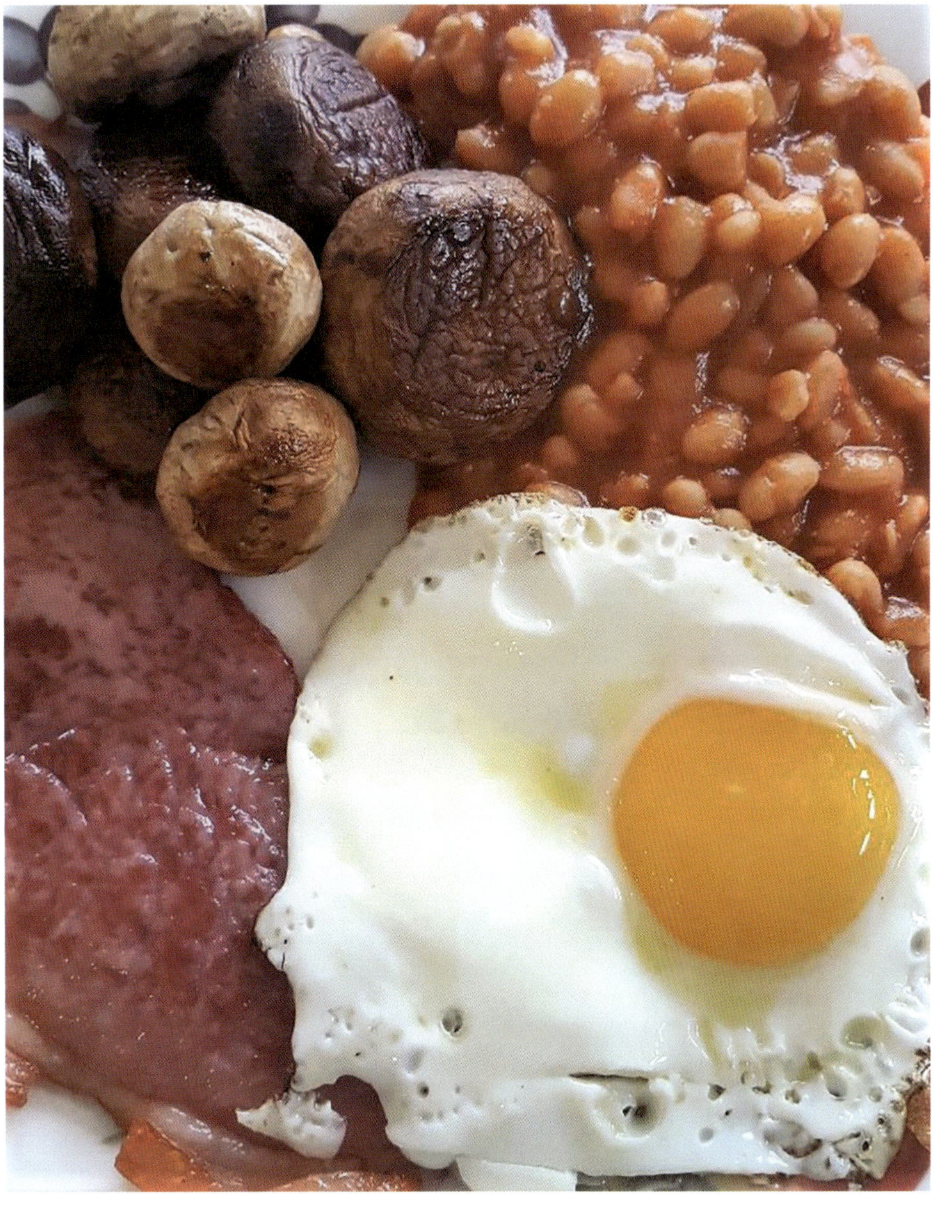

# Poached Eggs on Toast

Serves 1

*One of our favourite brunch snacks is poached eggs on toast. This has grown over time to include poached eggs on avocado on hummus on tomato on toast. Delicious, filling, simple to make and of course nutritious.*

Toast a slice of wholemeal bread. Spread with a generous portion of hummus, any preferred flavour. Slice a tomato and lay on top of the hummus, sprinkle with pepper. Slice an avocado and lay on top of the hummus. Top with two poached eggs and serve. The addition of a dash of Tabasco or chilli sauce spices it up.

### To poach the eggs:

Fill a saucepan with water and bring to the boil. Add a dessertspoonful of vinegar (not balsamic) to the water and reduce the heat. Break an egg into a small dish and taking a spoon swirl the water and drop the egg into the whirlpool. Leave to poach (an occasional bubble) for approximately 4-5 minutes until the white is set. Remove with a slotted spoon or fish slice and drain on a piece of kitchen towel before topping the avocado.

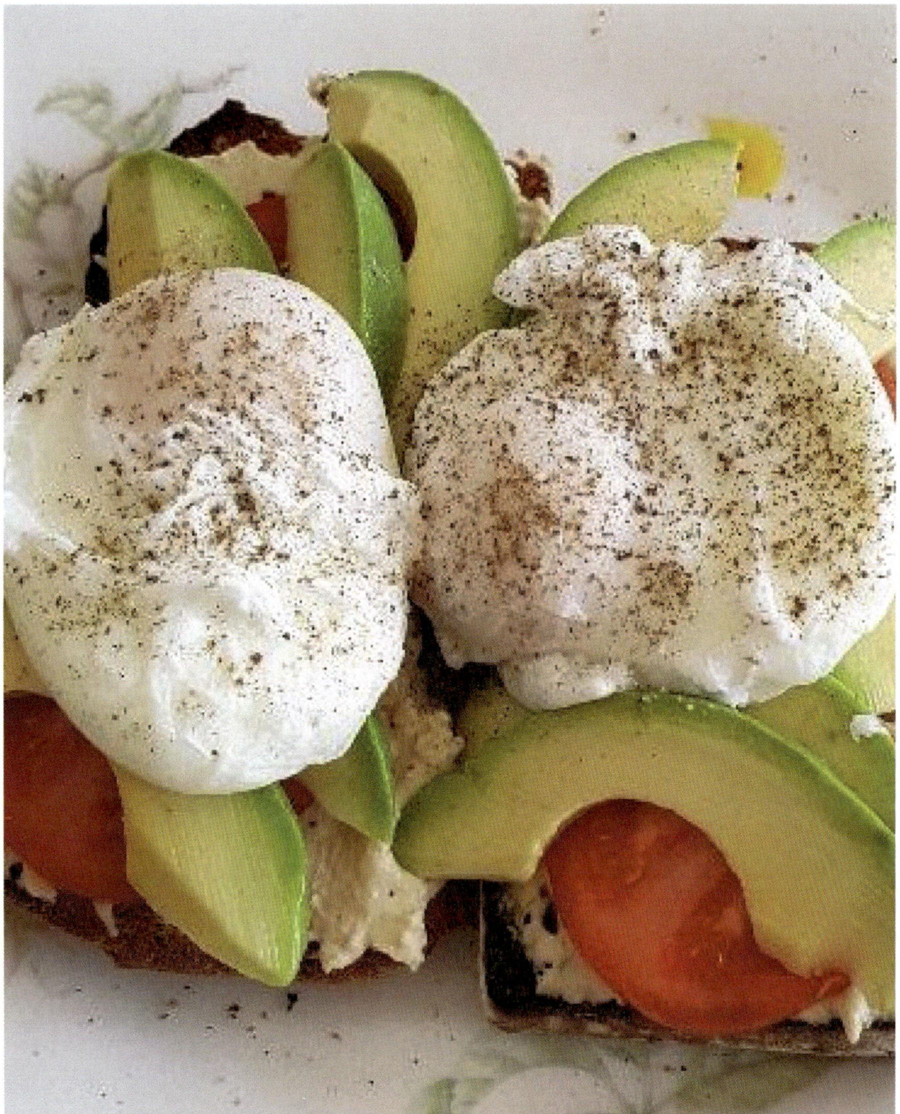

# Spiced Dried Fruit Salad

Serves 4-6

Dried fruit is a great standby if fresh fruits are getting low.  This fruit salad can be eaten for breakfast, hot or cold, with cereals, porridge, yoghurt and sprinkled with seeds and nuts.  If soaking overnight use a container with a lid just in case it gets a little rough.  Prunes can be cooked in exactly the same way if dried fruit salad is unavailable.  The flavour improves if kept for 24 hours once cooked and the liquid thickens.

*500 gms dried fruit salad*
*50 gms fresh ginger*
*1 lemon cut into 8 pieces*
*1 cinnamon stick*
*3 star anise*

Put the dried fruit and ginger into a container and cover with cold water*.  Leave to soak overnight.  Pour into a saucepan and bring to the boil.  Add the lemon, cinnamon stick and star anise to the pan, cover and simmer gently until the fruit is soft.  This should take approximately 20 minutes.  Serve hot or cold.

*I have found that if you want to cook the fruit salad immediately just cover with cold water and bring to the boil slowly.  When boiling, turn the heat down and simmer very gently.  You may find it takes a little longer to cook.

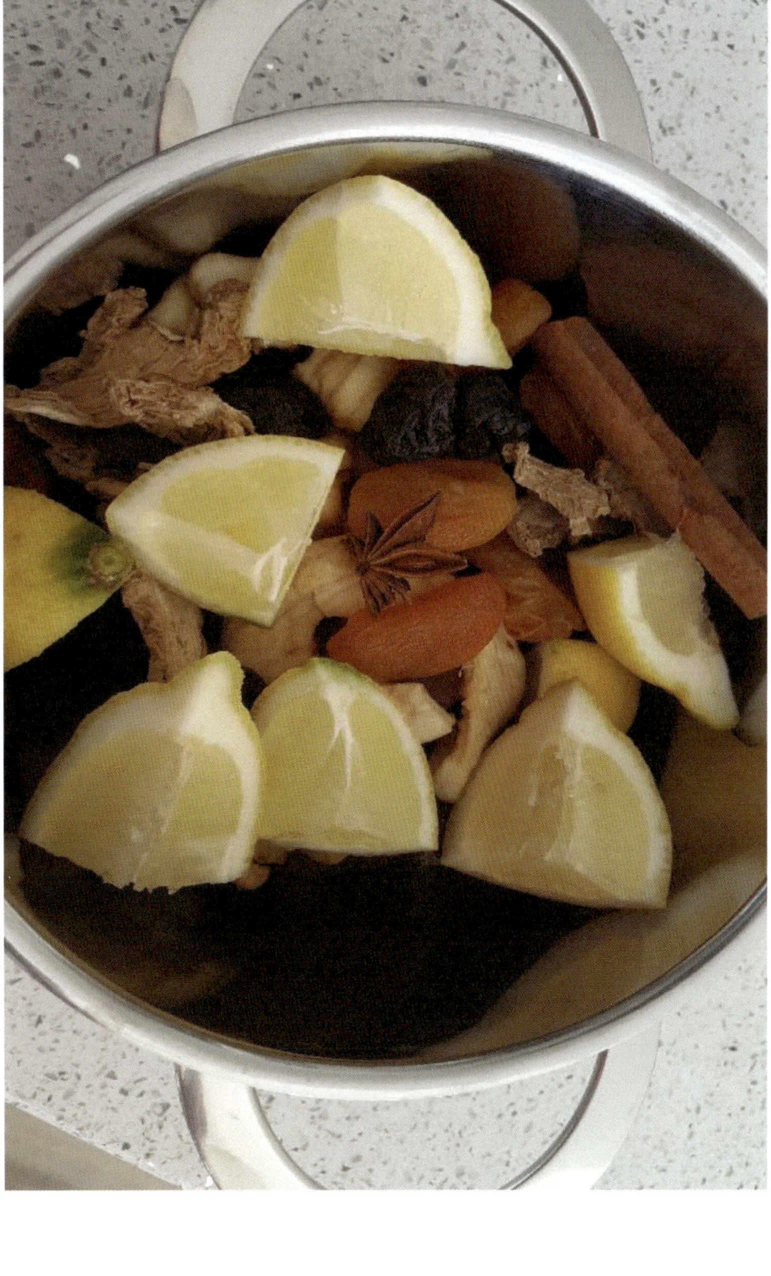

# Mushroom and Kale Eggs

Serves 1

A quick and delicious breakfast dish prepared and created by my lovely daughter.  It is something savoury and can be varied by using spinach  or other leafy greens if kale is unavailable.

Bring a saucepan of water to the boil.  Add a dessertspoonful of vinegar (not balsamic) to the water and reduce the heat.  Gently lower the egg into the water.  Boil for approximately 4-5 minutes.

Take 4 large flat mushrooms and fry quickly in hot oil in a frying pan.  Season and stack in the pan on one side to keep warm and add 2-3 handfuls of washed, chopped kale with some chopped garlic.  Cook quickly until softened.  Place the mushrooms on the plate, top with the kale which has been seasoned with salt and pepper.  Peel the boiled egg and place on top of the kale.  Serve with hummus and toast.

My daughter, inspirational and adventurous

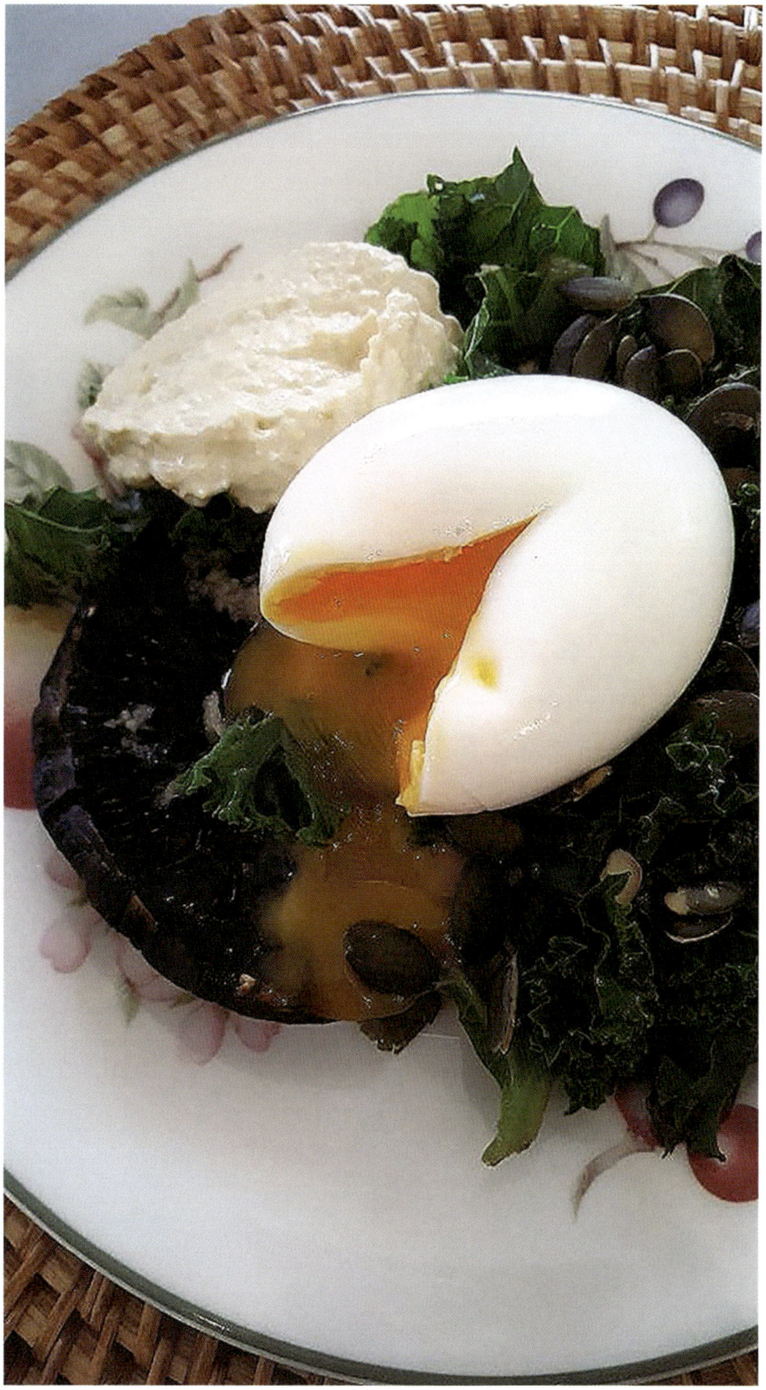

# Fresh Fruit Salad

Serves 4-6

This can be made up with whatever fruit you have on board but I have chosen a selection to provide colour and contrasting flavours.

*1 orange*

*1 kiwi fruit*

*1 apple*

*1 banana*

*Handful of blueberries*

*Handful of raspberries*

*Handful of strawberries*

*Handful of grapes*

*1/2 ripe melon*

*1 lemon*

*1 cm piece of fresh ginger*

Cut the fruit into spoon size pieces and place in a bowl. Squeeze the juice from the lemon and pour over the fruit. Grate the fresh ginger over the fruit. Mix the contents of the bowl well and serve with porridge, cereals or on its own with seeds, nuts and yoghurt.

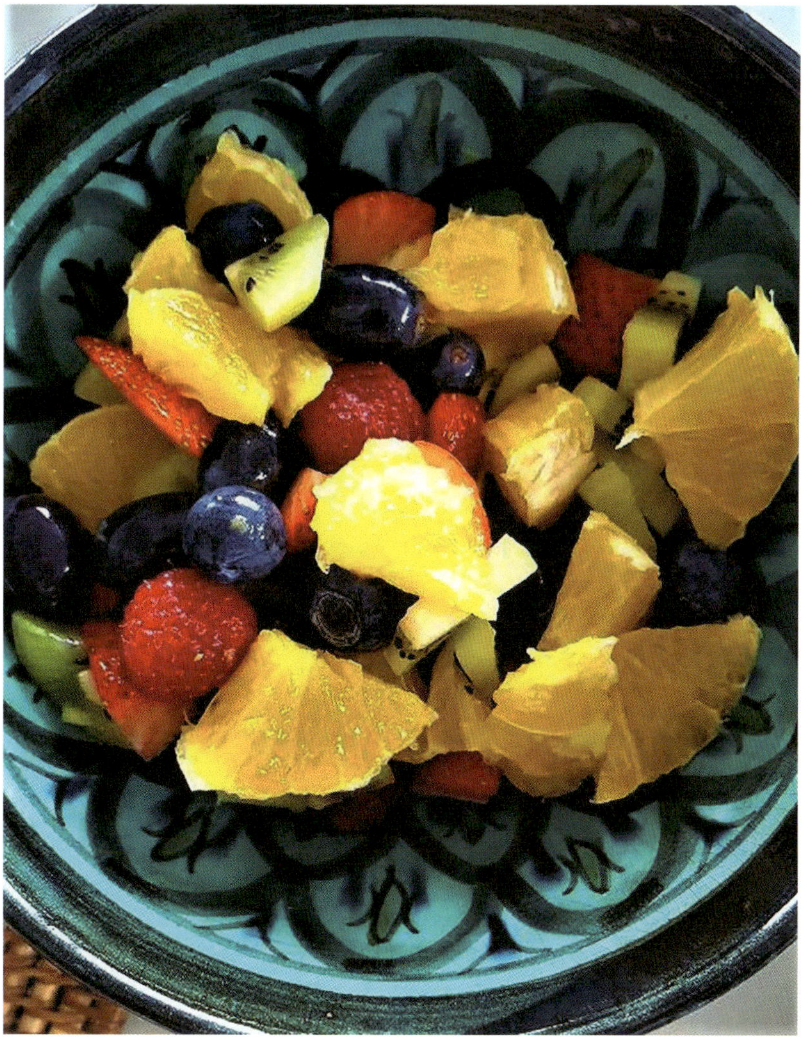

# Sunflower Banana Toast

Serves 1

This is a quickly prepared, filling and nourishing breakfast for crew that must have something to eat before getting underway. The variations are endless: the banana can be topped with chopped almonds, chopped hazelnuts, chia seeds, sultanas, yoghurt or desiccated coconut. Peanut butter, almond butter or tahini can be topped with mashed banana. For those with a sweet tooth use a chocolate hazelnut spread or lemon curd. Whatever you have in your store cupboard on board. It is delicious either on ordinary toast or bread but on a slice of Wheaty Fruit Loaf (page 146) it provides additional nutrition.

*1 banana per person*
*1 teaspoon sunflower seeds*
*1 teaspoon pumpkin seeds*
*2 slices of Wheaty Fruit Loaf (page 148) or wholemeal bread*

Mash the banana and spread on top of the slices of Wheaty Fruit Loaf, toast or bread. Sprinkle with the seeds and favourite topping and serve.

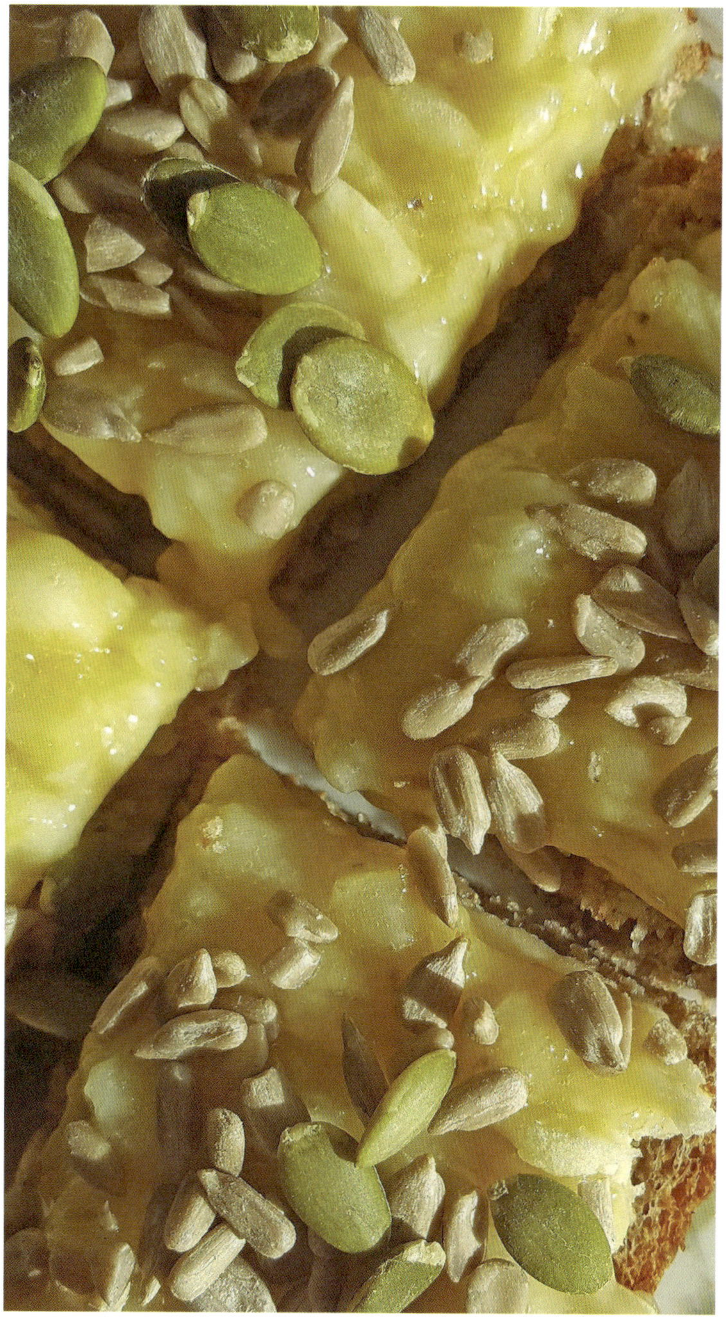

# Dawn Start Oats

Serves 1

"Time and tide wait for no man" reflects the nature of life at sea and on some mornings an early start is necessary to catch the tide.  Usually there is hardly time to make a hot drink before donning oil skins and reporting on deck ready for departure.  Preparation of breakfast the day before, in screw top transparent jars, is an ideal way to have a nourishing breakfast standing by when underway especially if it is a little choppy and being below for any length of time is unpleasant.

*¼ cup of oats or muesli*
*1 tbsp chia seeds*
*1 tbsp sunflower seeds*
*1 tbsp pumpkin seeds*
*milk*
*A handful of whole mixed nuts*
*Fruit: chopped apple, orange, mandarin segments, sliced strawberries, raspberries, sliced banana, sliced kiwi fruit*
*Yoghurt*

Put the oats in the bottom of a large jar with a screw lid.  Sprinkle with the chia seeds, sunflower seeds, pumpkin seeds and nuts.  Pour sufficient milk to cover the nuts.  The oats and chia seeds will soak up the milk.  Add a good serving of cut fresh fruit, cooked dried fruit salad or prunes. Remember that this is eaten from the jar so cut the fruit into bite sized pieces. Fill with yoghurt and screw on the lid being careful not to overfill.  Put in the fridge overnight.  Eat out of the jar the next day.  This is sufficient for one jar per person.

**NB:** Ensure you only fill your container ¾ full with ingredients and pour a generous amount of milk as the chia seeds and oats absorb a large amount of liquid.  These ingredients are only a guide and you can use what you have on board.

37

Evening at Crinan Harbour, Argyll and Bute, perfect for an evening swim

Kyles of Bute, Tighnabruaich after the rain

Passage through the Crinan Canal, Argyll and Bute, during a spell of bad weather

# Lunch

*Skipper hoping to catch lunch, Camel Estuary, Padstow*

Lunch on board depends on many variables; whether underway, alongside a berth, at anchor or swinging on a mooring in a comfortable anchorage. If underway the weather conditions dictate what to prepare and when. If rolling conditions are forecast preparing flasks of soup and sandwiches with the addition of crisps, fruit, biscuits or cake. Some of us find it difficult to go below and prepare food whilst underway and being thrown around. It isn't conducive to eating afterwards.

# Scrambled Eggs with Garlic and Smoked Salmon

### Serves 2-3

Spanish tapas give a delicious diversity of flavours from the variety available of both hot and cold dishes. They make an appetising alternative to the humble sandwich, which does have its place when you need to prepare lunch before setting off on a longer passage. Serve 2 or 3 tapas to add variety with fresh bread, olives, sun dried tomatoes and cured ham. I have included some of my favourites. This is a delicious quick tapa but it can also be a light supper dish or breakfast. This makes supper for 2 or combine with 4-6 different tapas as lunch for 4.

*2 cloves of garlic*
*3 spring onions*
*3 tablespoons olive oil*
*150g smoked salmon cut into strips*
*1 tablespoon milk*
*5 eggs*
*Toast or wholemeal bread*

Crush the garlic, trim and finely slice the spring onions. Heat the olive oil in a non-stick pan and cook the garlic and spring onions over a gentle heat until soft. Don't let the garlic burn.

Beat together the milk, eggs and a little pepper. Add the smoked salmon to the beaten eggs. Cook, stirring continuously until the eggs are creamy soft. Serve immediately on top of toast or wholemeal bread cut into squares.

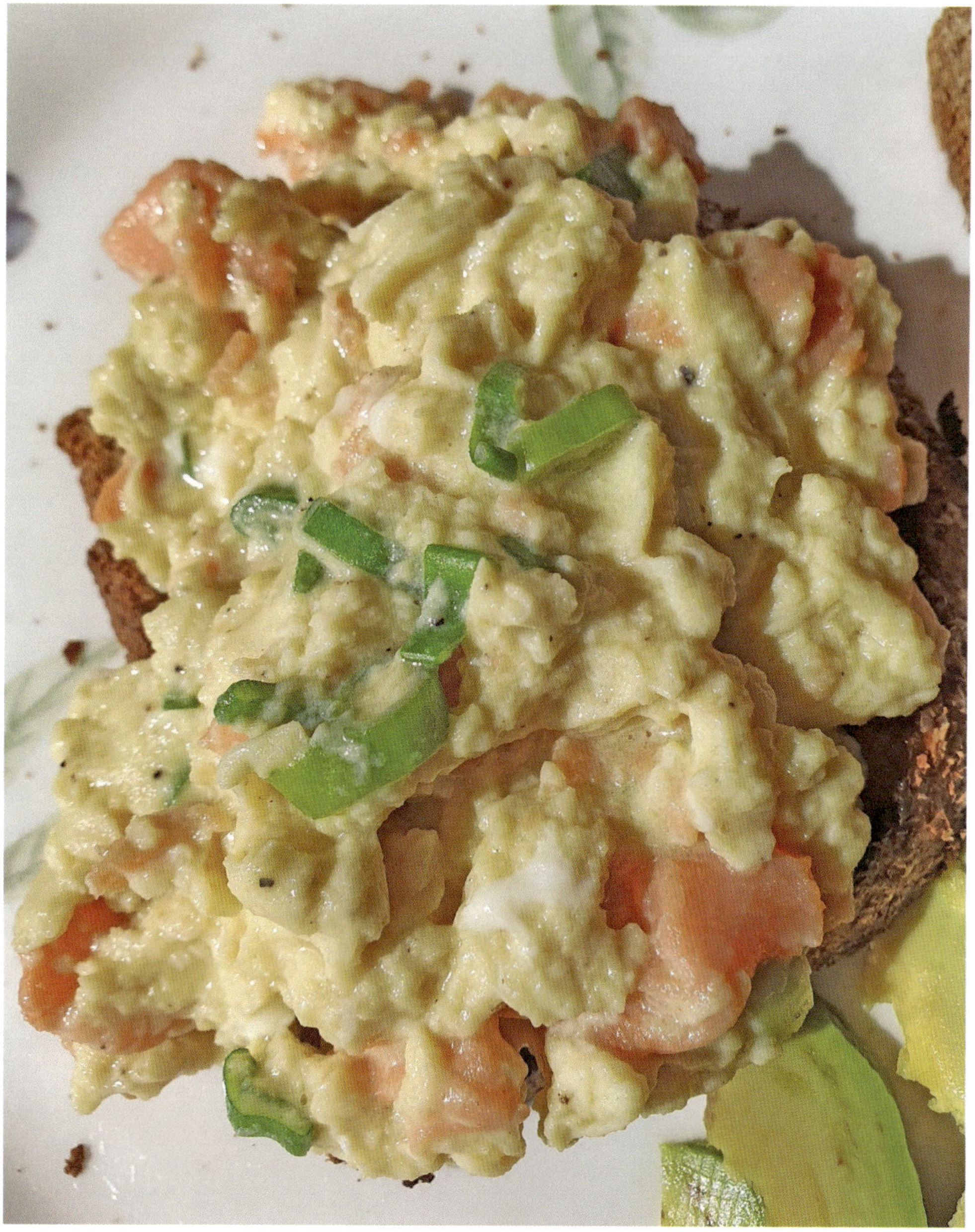

# Spinach with Raisins and Pine Nuts

Serves 2-3

A quick tapa delicious served with a Spanish omelette or scrambled eggs. Left over Spanish Lentils (page 80) or Spanish Chicken (page 78) can also be served as a tapa using up leftover meals and adding variety to lunch. It may seem a large quantity of spinach but it wilts down.

*1.5kg spinach*
*3 tablespoons of olive oil*
*50g pine nuts*
*2 cloves of garlic*
*80g seeded raisins*
*Slice of lemon*

Heat the oil in a large pan and fry the pine nuts until golden take out and put to one side. Add the chopped garlic and spinach to the pan and cook until the spinach wilts. Add the raisins, pepper and a squeeze of lemon. Stir in the pine nuts and serve

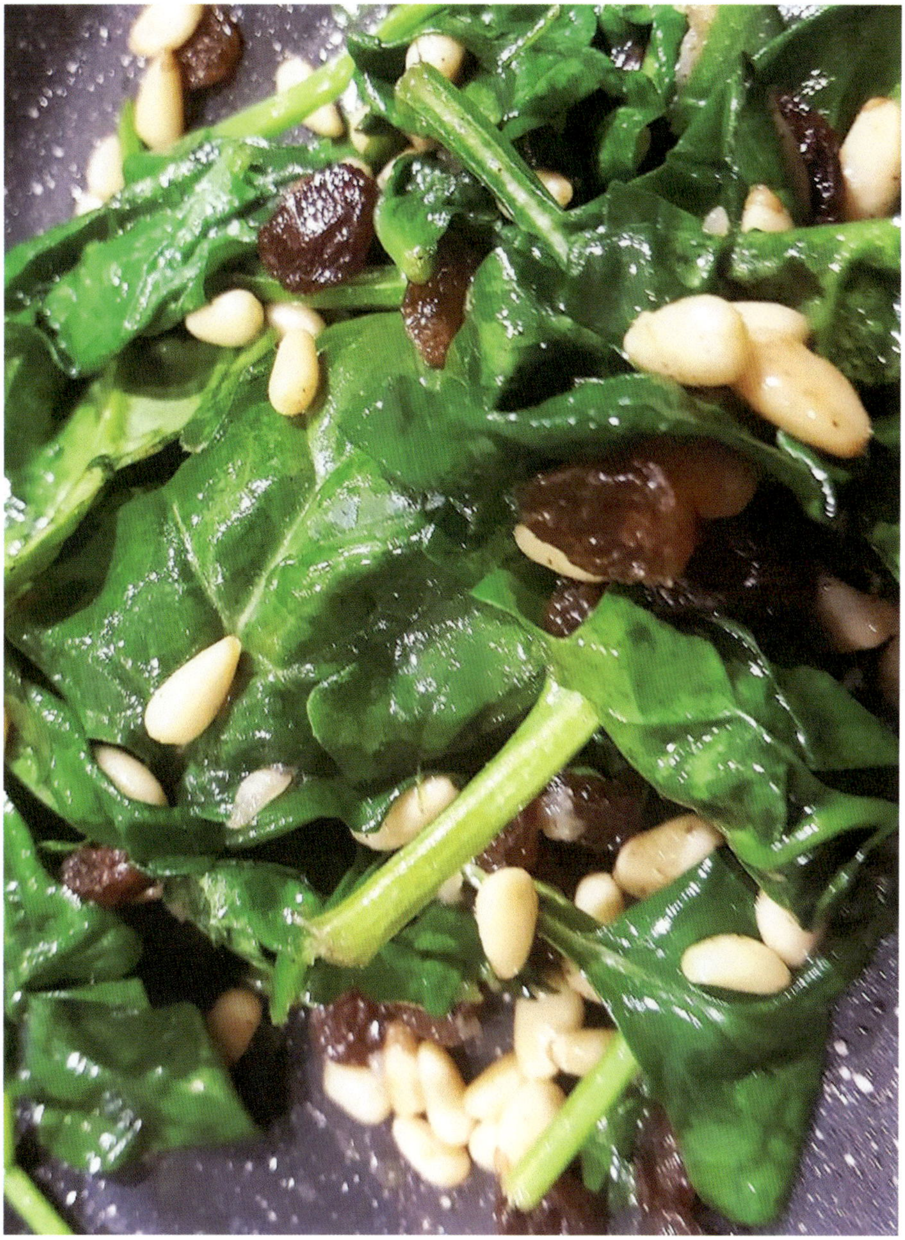

# Spanish Omelette

Serves 4

A Spanish omelette is a classic tapa which can be eaten either hot or cold.  As a child I remember the large Spanish family picnic where the omelette was placed whole, in a round flat loaf and cut into wedges.  Use leftover cooked potatoes to make this on board.

*6 tablespoons of olive oil*
*1 large onion, finely chopped*
*2 cloves of garlic crushed*
*500g cooked potatoes, cubed*
*6 eggs*

Heat the oil in a medium non-stick frying pan.  Add the onion and cook until transparent then add the crushed garlic, stir for 1 minute.  Add the cubed potatoes and mix together.  Beat the eggs and season with a little salt and pepper.  Pour over the onions and potatoes in the frying pan and cook over a medium heat gently bringing the sides into the centre until nearly set.  Shake the pan to keep the omelette from sticking.  When set, place a flat lid or plate over the top.  Hold tightly and turn the omelette over.  Add a little more oil to the pan and slide the omelette back into the frying pan.  Cook for a few minutes.  Slide onto a plate and serve hot or cold.

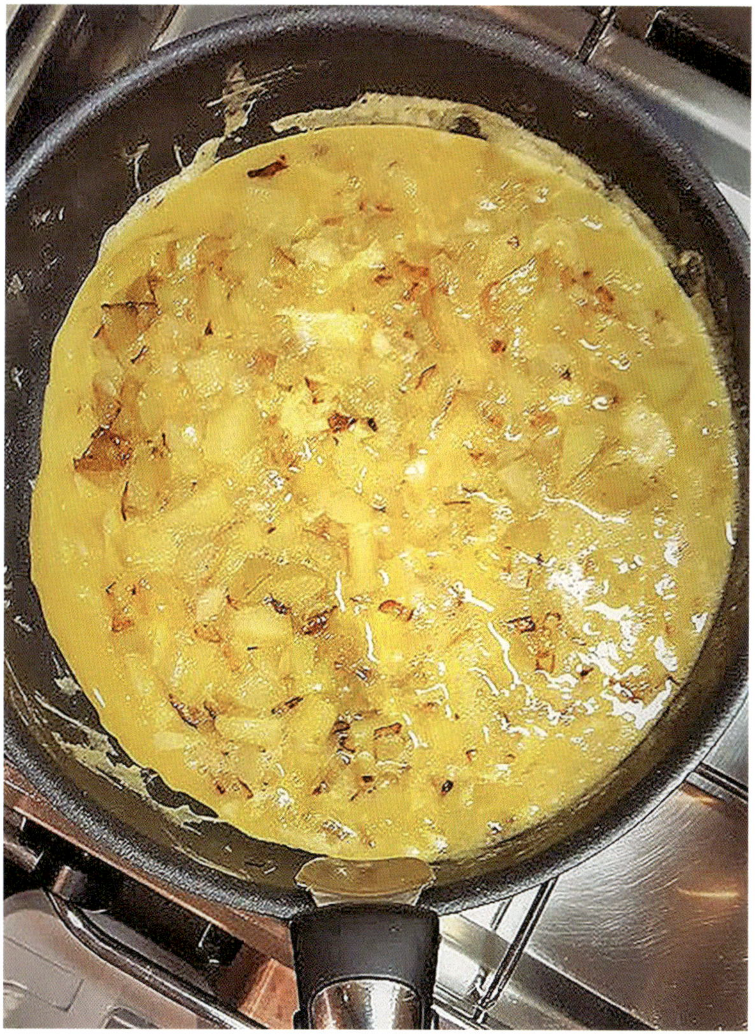

# The Humble Sandwich

When you are on passage making a batch of sandwiches is a failsafe way of having lunch to hand, and if it is cool, a flask of soup or coffee helps to keep those fingers and toes warm.

Preparing sandwiches on board always reminds me of a sailing holiday in Greece. Having to leave Kea to head back to Athens on the last two days of our holiday a Meltemi was blowing and choppy seas were deterring other sailors. It was a force 6 gusting 7 at times. As I headed for the supermarket, I noticed our neighbours in the marina left and on the way back to the yacht noticed them heading back to the marina. However, we decided to pack some food and head out knowing we could always return if the conditions were impossible. The yacht slammed down in the troughs and rose up on the waves, but we got to the top of the island and were able to hoist our sails and headed for Perdika on Aegina.

We arrived as the sun was setting the wind having blown itself out and enjoyed a refreshing swim. The sandwiches were enjoyed as we sailed, and I was relieved I didn't have to go below, in a very uncomfortable sea to prepare food.

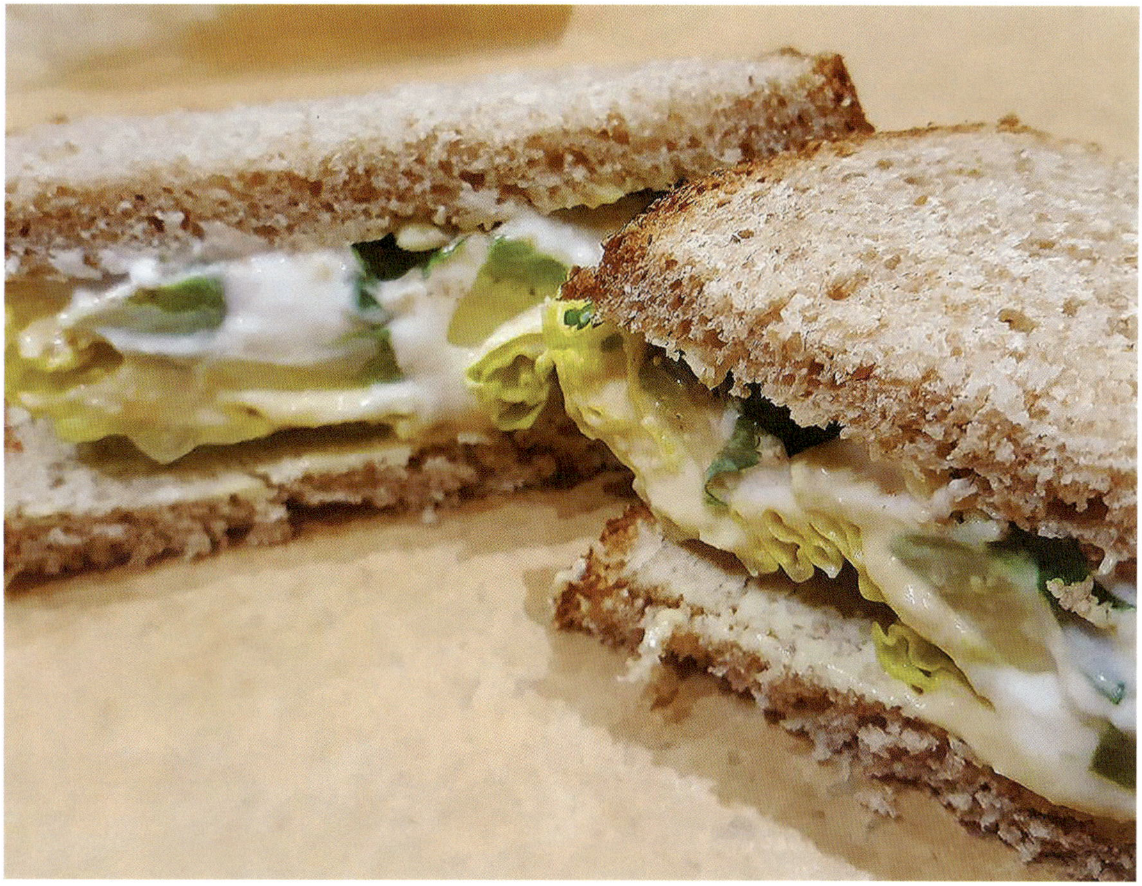

# Open or Closed Sandwiches

When conditions are peaceful or at anchor a nutritious way of preparing sandwiches and halving the amount of bread but doubling the filling, is an open sandwich. The slice of bread acts like a plate and a variety of different toppings make this an inventive way of eating a sandwich. A base is always a good way to start and the sandwich can be built from that. To make a closed sandwich when packing a lunch or if it is rough just add a slice of buttered bread on top and maybe not quite so much filling.

## Tomato Base

Cut a tomato into fine slices and arrange on top of the buttered slice of bread. The following toppings are suggestions that complement the base.

- Sardines, black olives, a drizzle of oil and torn fresh basil leaves and slices of onion
- Wafer thin ham, Dijon mustard and a sprinkle of snipped coriander
- Ham, finely sliced gem lettuce with a spoonful of mayonnaise and snipped chives
- Grated cheese, a spoonful of red coleslaw (page 66) and snipped chives or finely sliced spring onion
- Crumbled feta cheese, small cubes of cucumber and black olives with a drizzle of olive oil
- Rub the bread with a slice of garlic before adding the slice tomatoes, arrange anchovies and olives, finish with slices of onion, and chopped fresh herbs such as parsley or dill. Drizzle with olive oil.
- Roasted Mediterranean vegetables topped with cannellini beans seasoned with finely chopped onion, dill, olive oil and lemon juice
- Sliced brie sprinkled with chopped spring onion and fresh dill

## Cucumber Base

- Cut enough fine slices of cucumber to cover the slice of bread. The following toppings are suggestions that complement the base.

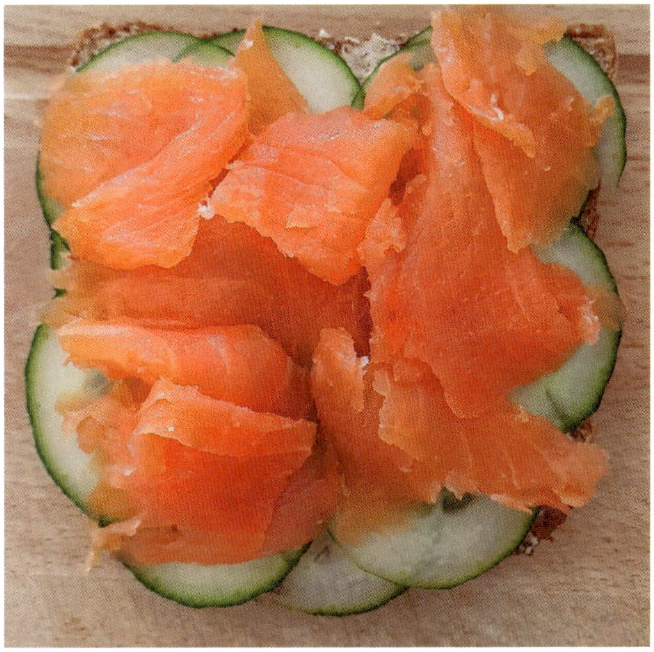

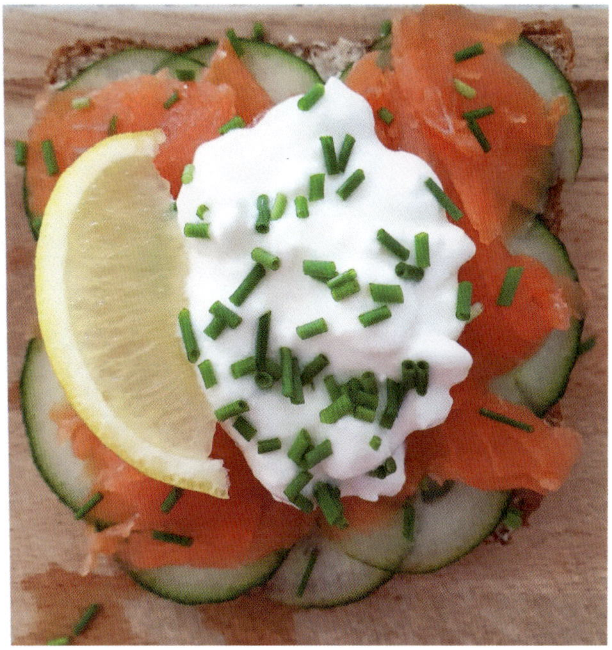

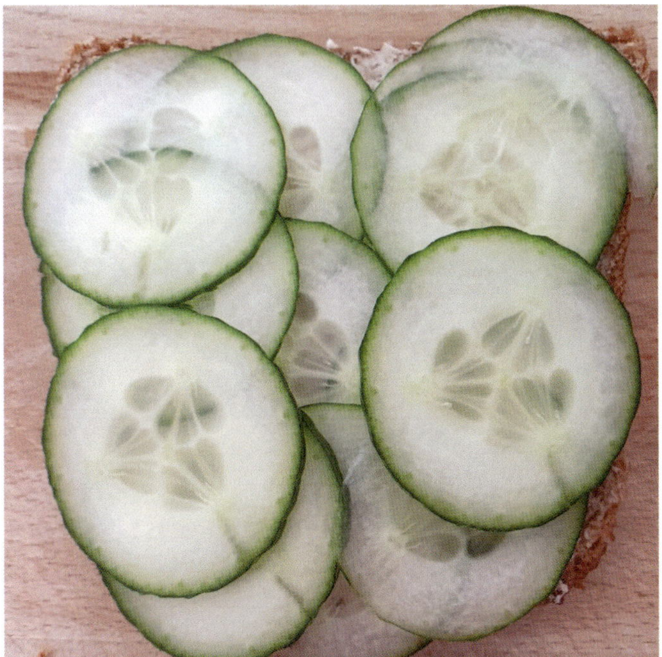

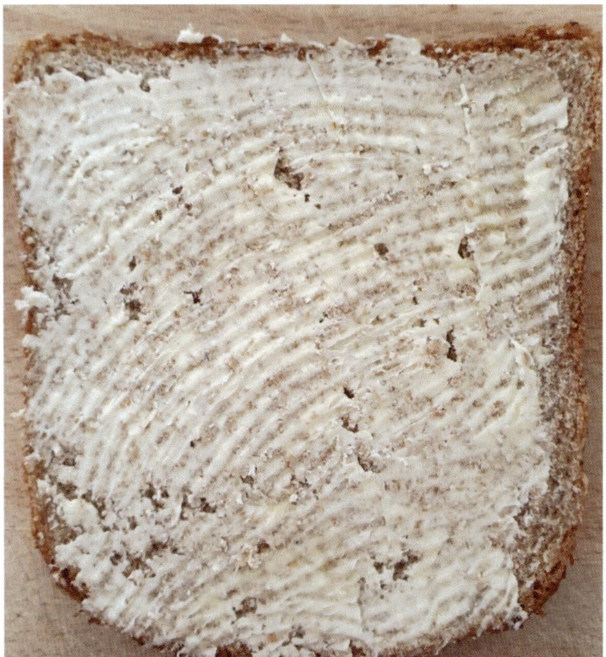

# Open or Closed Sandwiches Continued

- Smoked salmon with cream or cottage cheese, a wedge of lemon and snipped chives
- Cheese slices, wafer thin ham, a spoonful of chutney and chopped fresh coriander
- Feta cheese crumbled with black olives, chopped tomato, slices of onion and chopped mint
- Flaked, cooked fresh salmon, a spoonful of mayonnaise a wedge of lemon and fresh dill
- No Drain tuna, sliced hard-boiled egg, chopped tomato, slices of onion and a spoonful of mayonnaise or a drizzle of oil and squeeze of lemon juice

**Lettuce or Watercress Base**

- Sliced hardboiled egg topped with slices of avocado, a large spoonful of hummus and a teaspoonful of pesto
- Prawns coated in Marie Rose sauce (mayonnaise or plain yoghurt, tomato ketchup, a dash of tabasco and a squeeze of lemon) sprinkled with fresh dill and chopped tomato
- Cooked chicken coated in a sauce made of mayonnaise or plain yoghurt, mango chutney and a dash of chilli sauce with slices of tomato and onion
- Ham with slices of tomatoes, sliced mushrooms, a large spoonful of mayonnaise or plain yoghurt and snipped parsley
- Scrambled egg with strips of smoked salmon and sprinkled with sniped chives
- Hummus topped with sliced avocado and a spoonful of plain yoghurt sprinkled with paprika and torn coriander
- Avocado sliced and topped with finely sliced red pepper and topped with pesto
- Coleslaw topped with crumbled cheese, wafer thin ham, sliced tomato and slices of apple

53

# Sweet Sandwiches

*There are times when the perfect end to a meal is something sweet. Here are some suggestions for sweet sandwiches where the base can be a slice of cake, banana bread, panettone, bara brith, Welsh cakes, a scotch pancake, stollen or gingerbread. Use what you have on board and if it is a little dry this is an ideal way to use it up.*

- Peanut butter topped with blackcurrant jam and sprinkled with blueberries
- Cottage cheese topped with sliced strawberries, strawberry jam and torn mint leaves
- Chocolate spread topped with raspberries and blueberries and a large spoonful of coconut yoghurt, sprinkled with granola
- Slices of banana topped with spoonfuls of crème caramel or cold custard and sprinkle with cinnamon
- Apple or rhubarb puree generously sprinkled with granola and a spoonful of cold custard
- Mascarpone cheese or crème fraîche topped with cherry jam, raspberries and passionfruit
- Lemon curd folded into coconut yoghurt topped with raspberries, coconut shavings or desiccated coconut, torn mint and grated lime
- Layer of raspberry jam topped with ground almonds folded into coconut yoghurt and sprinkled with flaked almonds

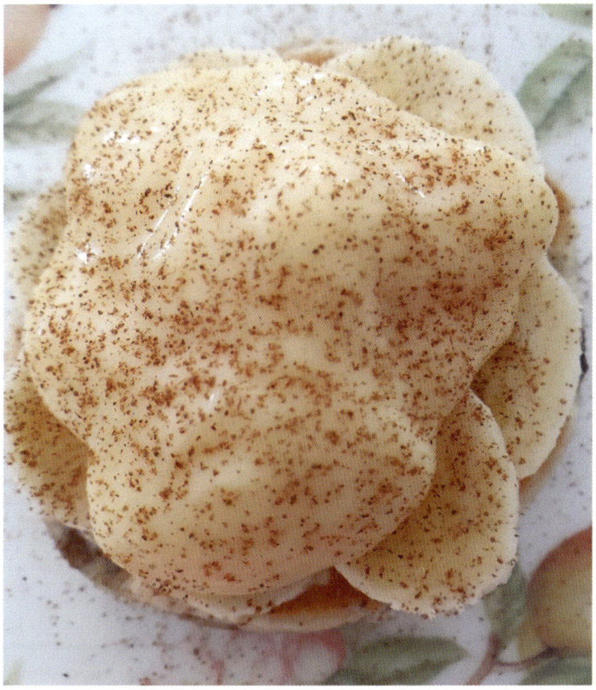
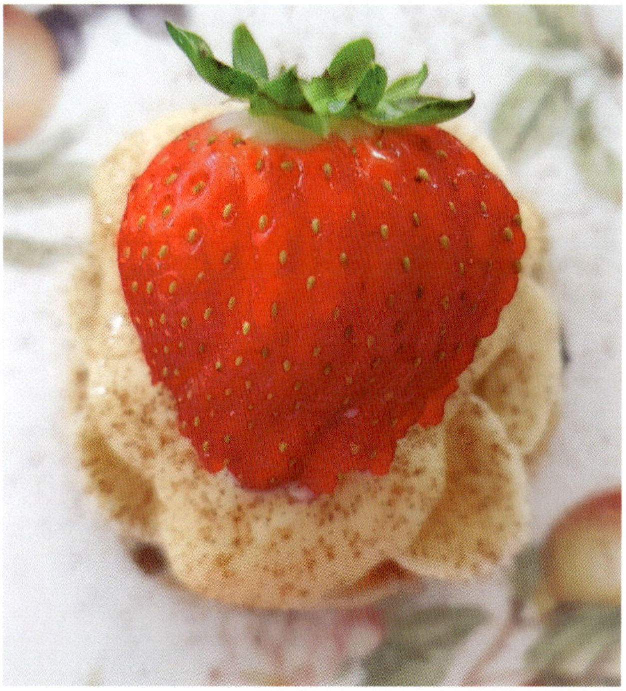
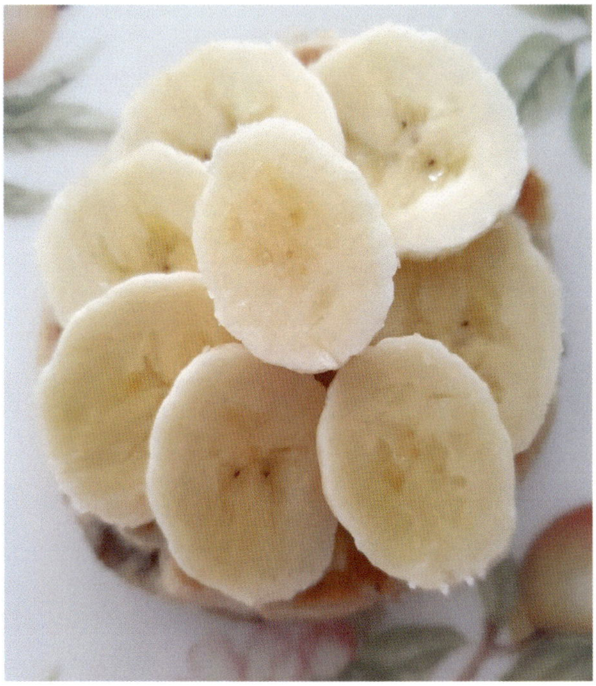
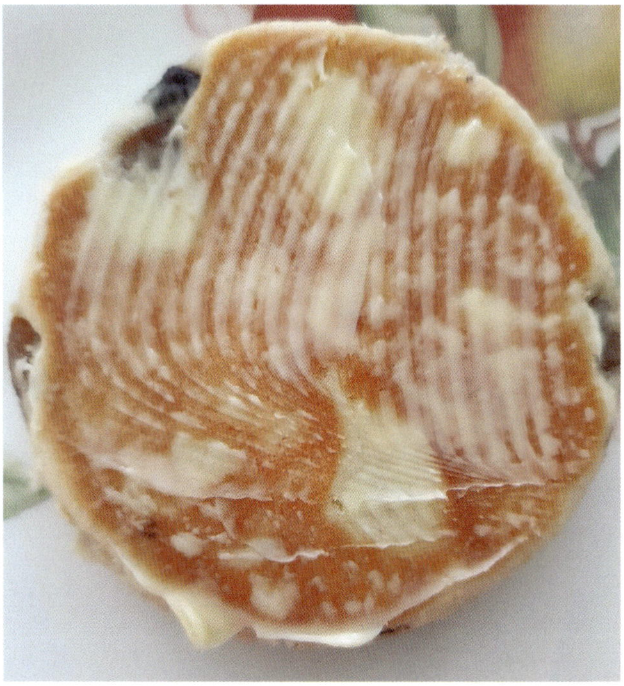

# Spinach and Pesto Quiche

Serves 4-6

A quiche is a perfect lunch dish if you are alongside or on a mooring. Serve with a salad to add crunch and contrast to a delicious meal. You will need to make a crust by using the recipe Quick Pastry Crust in the baking section (page 160) and prepare it to the stage where it has been baked blind. Be careful not to overfill as the liquid can spill when placing in the oven.

*1 Quick Pastry Crust baked blind (page 160)*
*3 eggs*
*250 ml milk*
*250g feta*
*1 500g bag of washed spinach*
*I small onion, finely chopped*
*1 tablespoon olive oil*
*2 cloves garlic, crushed*
*2 tablespoons green pesto or a handful of chopped basil*
*Grated cheese*
*Pepper*

Heat the olive oil in a medium saucepan, add the onion and soften until transparent. Add the garlic and spinach and cook over a low heat until the spinach is wilted. Squeeze out any surplus water with a fork and leave to drain in a colander. Cut the feta into small cubes and sprinkle over the pastry case base. Return the drained spinach to the saucepan, stir in the green pesto, mix well and spoon over the feta. Beat the eggs together and add the milk and pepper to taste. Place the quiche dish on a tray and pour in the egg and milk over the spinach, don't over fill. Sprinkle the top with grated cheese. Bake in a moderate oven 180°C, 160°C fan, Gas 4, for 30—35 minutes until the quiche is set and the top is browned a little. Leave to cool for 15 minutes before serving. Can be served hot or cold

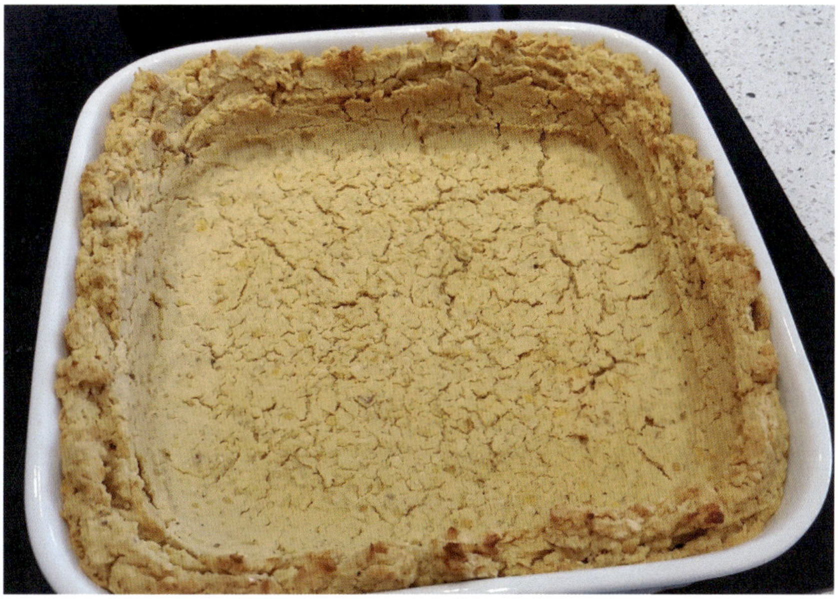

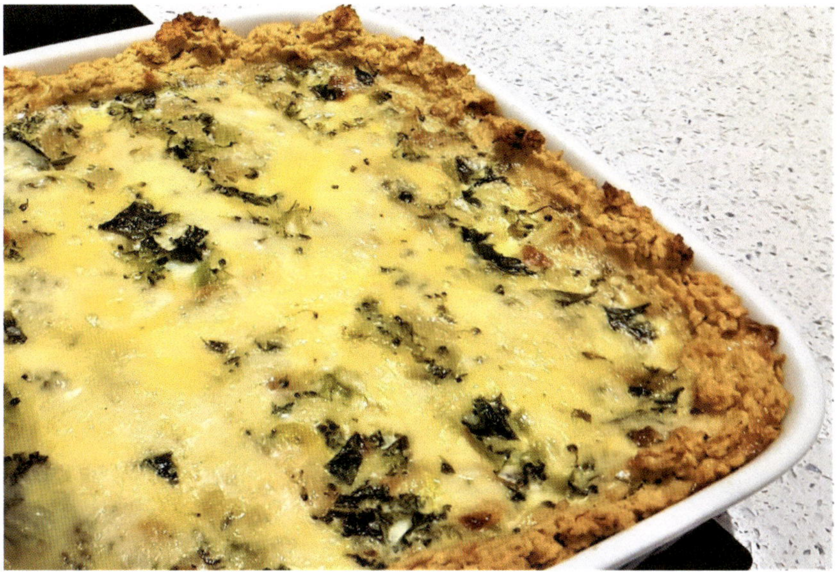

# Bean Tabbouleh with Hummus

*Serves 4*

Tabbouleh is a delicious salad which can be quickly made on board and makes a satisfying lunch with hummus and bread. It can be varied according to personal taste and ingredients in your provisions locker. I use nutty cracked wheat but couscous works just as well. While the bulgur (cracked wheat) is soaking you can prepare the other ingredients and then combine. Be generous with the mint it adds a wonderful flavour. Pitta bread is a perfect accompaniment and the pocket can be filled with hummus and salad if underway to make it easier to eat. There is a wonderful selection of shop bought hummus to choose from and usually little time or equipment to make your own.

*125g bulgur (cracked wheat)*
*1 onion, finely chopped*
*3 tomatoes, finely chopped*
*¼ of a cucumber, finely chopped*
*1 avocado, cut into small cubes*
*1 400g tin of cannellini beans, drained*
*1 lemon*
*2 tablespoons olive oil*
*Fresh mint, finely chopped*
*Parsley, finely chopped*
*Ground pepper*
*6 large pitta bread*
*2 large 300g pots hummus*

Put the bulgur in a bowl and cover with hot water. Leave for 30 minutes while you prepare the remainder of the salad ingredients. Put all the chopped and cubed ingredients in a salad bowl with the cannellini beans. Add the chopped mint and parsley and finally the drained and squeezed bulgur. Stir in lemon juice, olive oil and pepper to season. Mix well. Place the pitta bread on a tray and put in a hot oven for 10 minutes covered with foil so they don't dry out. Cut in half and serve with the tabbouleh and hummus.

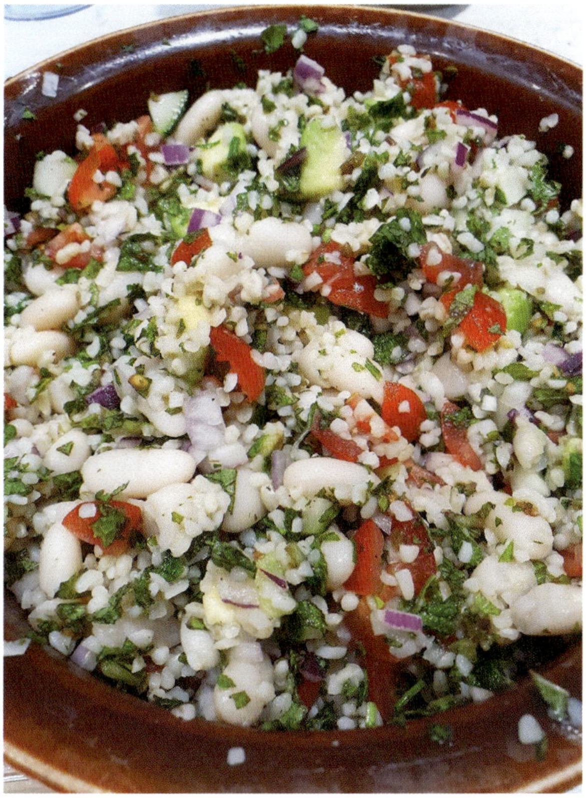

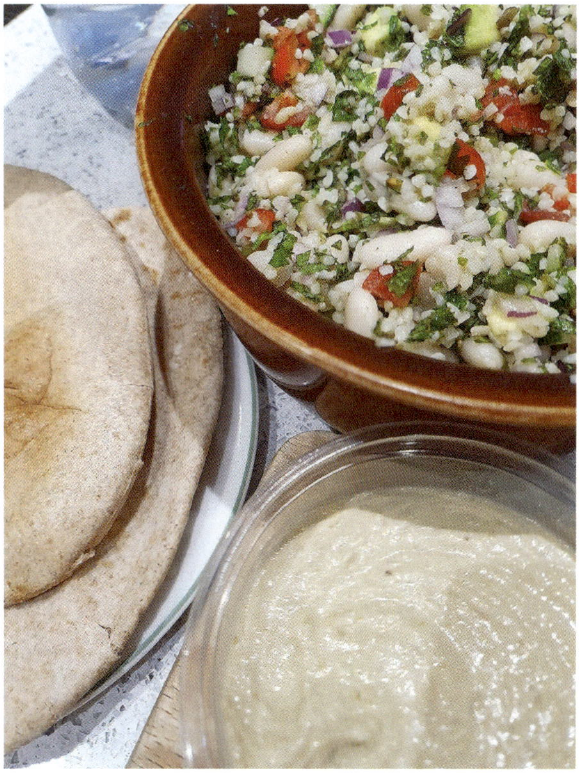

# Huevos Rancheros

Serves 4

This is a variation on a popular egg dish and can be made with Spanish Lentils. You can omit the chorizo if you wish. Simply add a chopped chilli and fried sliced peppers to the lentil mixture. If there are left over Spanish Lentils (page 80) it is an ideal way to use them up especially if there isn't quite enough for another meal. They can be spooned into a baking dish with the eggs and baked in the oven while you anchor for lunch.

*2 red peppers, sliced*
*1 green chilli, chopped*
*Olive oil*
*Green olives*
*1 tin of chopped tomatoes*
*1 or 2 eggs per person*
*Half the quantity of lentils in the Spanish Lentils recipe (Page 80)*

Heat the oven to 180° C, 160°C fan, Gas 4. Heat 2-3 tablespoons of olive oil in a saucepan and add the sliced red peppers. Cook these over a moderate heat until they are soft, add the chopped chilli. Add the lentil mixture with a tin of tomatoes and bring to the boil. When hot pour the mixture into an oven proof dish. Make a well in the lentil mixture large enough to take an egg and enough wells for the number of eggs to be added. Break the eggs into a cup and then transfer them into the wells in the lentil mixture. Scatter olives over the dish and place in the oven. Bake until the eggs are just set. This usually takes 15-20 minutes. Serve on its own or with a green salad.

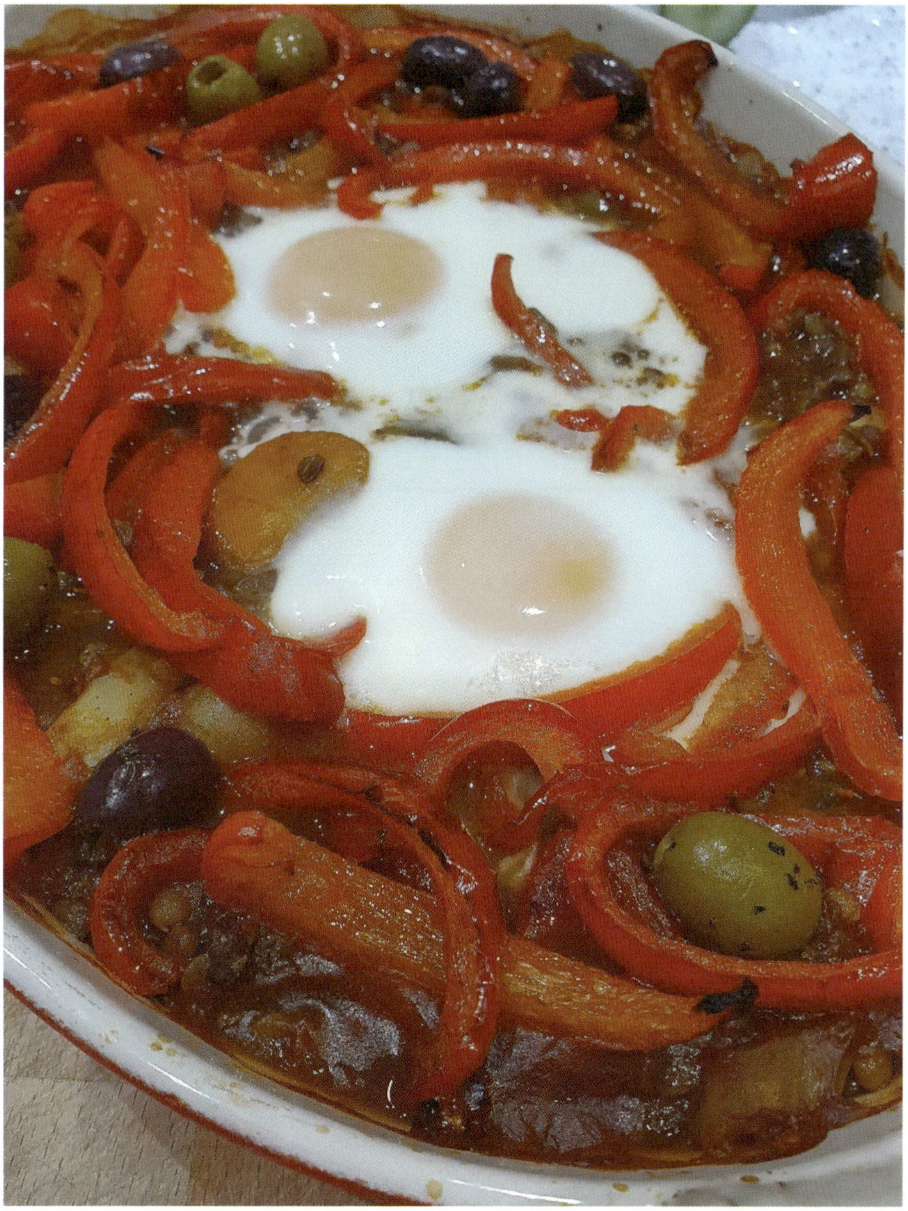

Torre de San Nicholás, entrance to Vieux Port, La Rochelle

# Salads and Vegetables

## Serve as a main or side dish

# Tuna Salad
Serves 1

I made this one lunch time when we had stopped off Dragonera, Mallorca having left Port d'Andratx that morning. There had been a terrible storm the night before and we had been up most of the night making sure that boats dragging their anchors didn't wrap around ours. We anchored in a small bay and enjoyed a late Spanish lunch of this salad with bread and a small glass of wine. If tides allow a short siesta is recommended. Having provisioned we left for Port de Sóller, the only safe harbour on the north west coast of Mallorca. The ingredients act as a guide. Use what you have on board.

Ingredients per person:
*1 60g tin No Drain tuna in oil*
*1 egg per person*
*½ gem lettuce*
*4 baby plum tomatoes*
*1 x 3 cm piece of cucumber*
*½ avocado*
*6 Olives*
*Slices of onion*
*Olive oil*
*Vinegar or lemon juice*
*Salt and pepper*
*Mustard (optional)*

Put egg into a saucepan, cover with cold water, bring to the boil and cook for 5 minutes. Cool the egg quickly in cold water, peel and leave in cold water until ready to use. Wash the lettuce, tomatoes and cucumber. Tear the lettuce into pieces and put into a salad bowl with the halved baby plum tomatoes, cucumber slices cut into quarters and onion slices. Peel the avocado and cut into chunks, add to the bowl together with some olives. Mix together 1 tablespoon of vinegar or lemon juice, half a teaspoon of mustard, pinch of salt and pepper until combined. Add 3 tablespoons of oil and mix well with a fork until it becomes an emulsion. Pour over the salad and mix well. Put chunks of tuna on top of the salad and decorate with the hard-boiled egg cut into four. Serve with bread (and that small glass of wine).

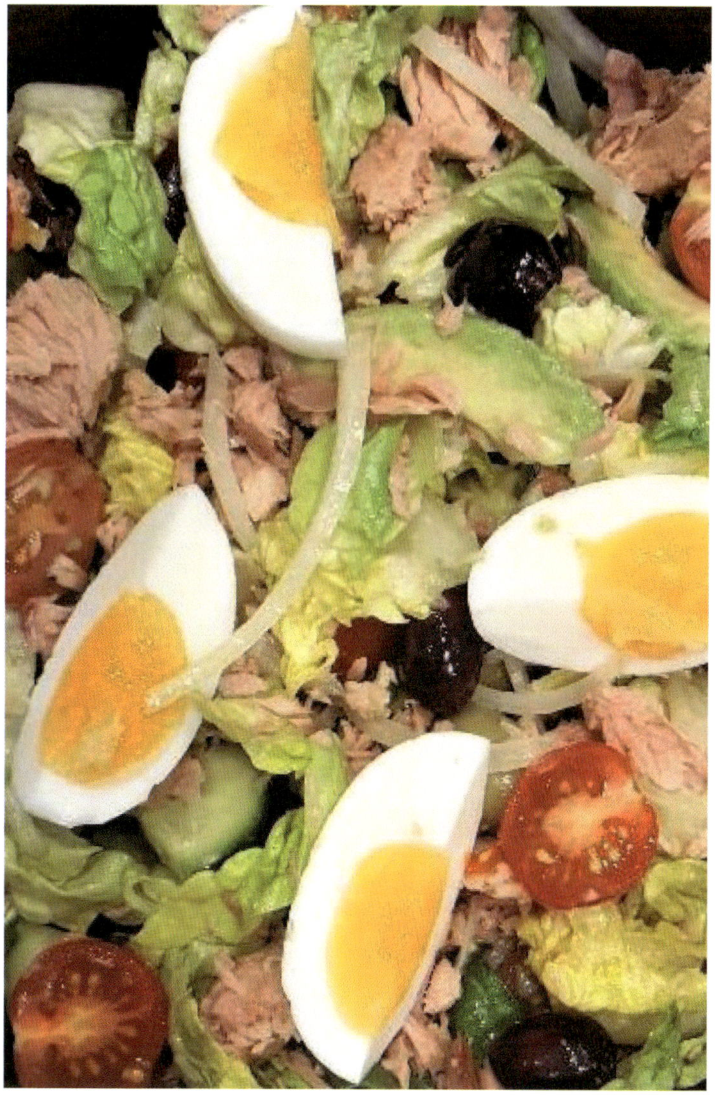

# Mixed Salad

Serves 2

No meal is complete, in my opinion, without a salad or a selection of vegetables. Not only for the contrast of colour and flavours but also for their nutritional value. There are many combinations of ingredients that can be included in a salad and I have chosen a selection of my favourites.

*1 ripe avocado, cut into cubes*
*5 radishes, sliced*
*3 button mushrooms, sliced*
*6 slices of cucumber, cut into quarters*
*12 cherry tomatoes, cut in half*
*2 spring onions, sliced*
*½ bag ready washed baby spinach*
*Dijon Mustard*
*Salt and pepper*
*Olive oil and cider vinegar*

Put all the prepared salad ingredients into a salad bowl. Mix a teaspoon of Dijon mustard with salt, pepper and 1 tablespoon of vinegar. To this add 3 tablespoons of olive oil and whisk well together until it is all combined. Pour into the bottom of the salad bowl and mix in when ready to serve.

# Red Coleslaw

**This is a salad that improves with keeping for a couple of days**

Finely shred a quarter of a red cabbage and add a grated dessert apple, a finely chopped onion and a grated carrot. Mix well with a tablespoon of olive oil, a tablespoon of cider vinegar, 1 teaspoon of English mustard and 4 tablespoons of plain unsweetened yoghurt. Serve as a side salad or in sandwiches.

67

# Quinoa Salad

Serves 2

**This is a healthy, satisfying and unusual salad that can be made very quickly whilst at anchor or when underway weather permitting.**

Take 2 thick slices of butternut squash and cut into small cubes. Place in a frying pan with 1 tablespoon of olive oil and cook stirring occasionally until softened and golden. There is no need to peel the butternut squash. Leave to cool. Cook half a cup of quinoa in enough water to cover for 10 minutes. Drain and leave to cool.

Meanwhile wash a bunch of watercress and drain, halve some cherry tomatoes and add to a salad bowl with the watercress. Cut 1 ripe, peeled avocado into cubes and add. Finely slice a red onion and add to the salad bowl.

Combine the cooled quinoa and butternut squash with the ingredients in the salad bowl and sprinkle generously with pomegranate. Drizzle a little olive oil over the salad and serve with wedges of lemon and wholemeal bread.

### Variation on a theme:

- You can top the salad with nuts such as cashews, peanuts or pistachio
- Sprinkle a seed mix over the salad for extra crunch
- Add a can of cannellini beans which have been tossed in crushed garlic and olive oil
- Sprinkle with crumbled feta cheese
- Add small cubes of watermelon

69

# Fennel and Orange Salad

Serves 2

The sweet aniseed flavour of fennel combined with the acidity of sliced orange is a wonderful way to eat this vegetable.  The pomegranate introduces a beautiful colour contrast and evokes a Mediterranean flavour to your meal as well as providing many health benefits.  A simple dressing of oil and vinegar will not overpower the delicate flavours.

*1 large or 2 small fennel bulbs*
*2 oranges*
*¼ of a pomegranate*
*Olive oil and vinegar*

Cut the green shoots from the fennel bulb and slice the fennel bulb finely.  The green stalks can be added to a soup or stew.  Peel the orange and slice thinly into rounds.  Place in a salad bowl with the fennel.  Remove the pomegranate seeds and add to the salad.  To 1 tablespoon of light vinegar add a little salt and pepper.  Add 3 tablespoons of olive oil and whisk well until combined.  Pour into the bottom of the salad bowl and mix in when ready to serve.

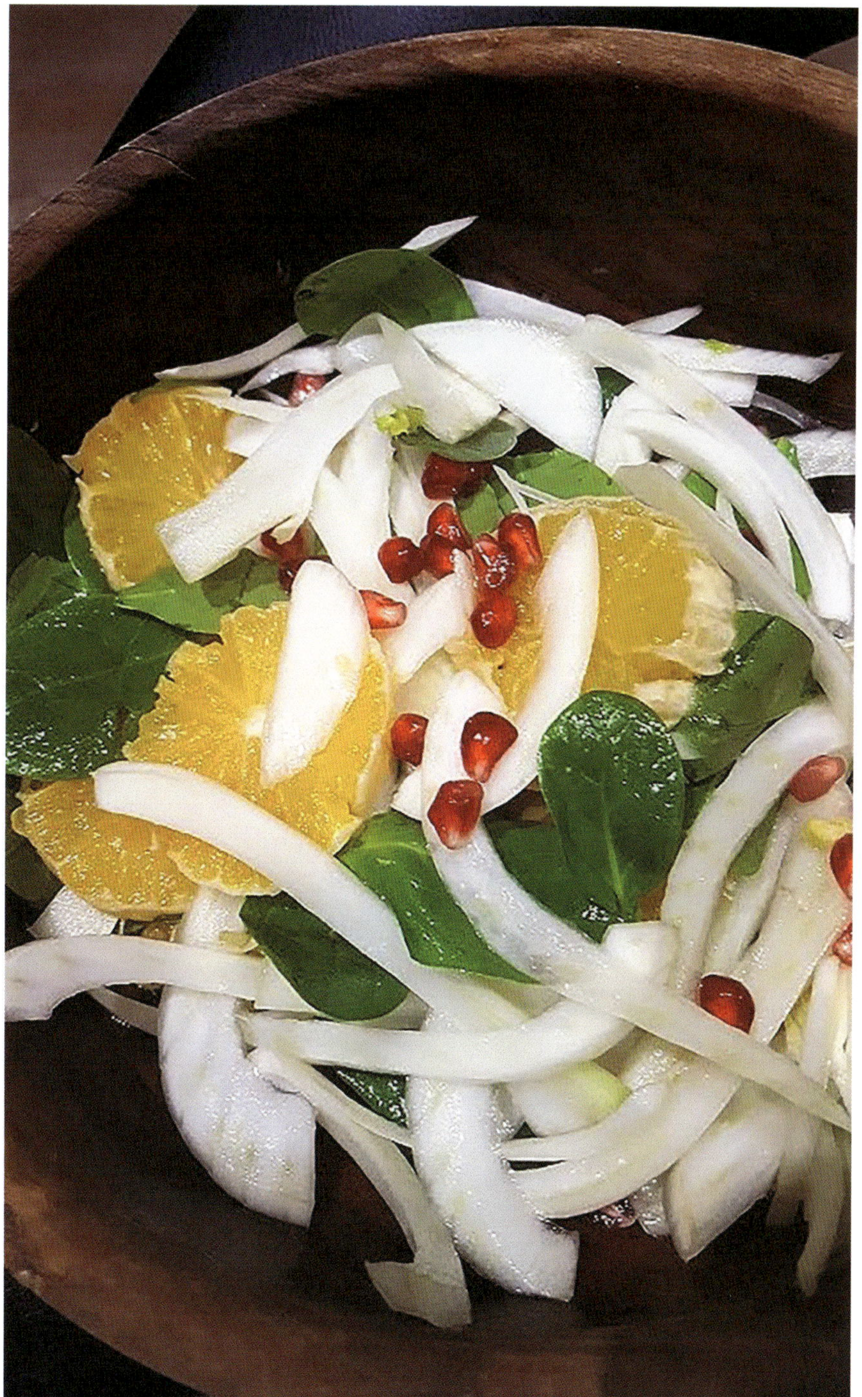

# Green Vegetable Stir Fry

Serves 4

When leaving the yacht for any length of time or using up what is left before re-provisioning there will be a time when vegetables need to be used up and a stir fry is a perfect way to do this. Add the vegetables in order of cooking time with the longest at the start and say spinach right at the end.

*1 head of broccoli, trimmed into small florets*
*1 pack of mangetout*
*1 bag spinach*
*2 courgettes, cut into cubes*
*1 onion, sliced*
*3 – 4 tbsp olive oil*
*2-3 cloves of garlic, crushed*
*2 tsps cornflour*
*Vegetable bouillon*
*Soy sauce*
*Chilli sauce, sweet or hot according to preference*

Prepare all the vegetables before starting to cook. Put the cornflour into a bowl and stir in 2 tablespoons of soy sauce, one of chilli sauce and 2 tablespoons of warm water to which 1 teaspoon of vegetable bouillon has been added. Heat the oil in a saucepan large enough to take the combined vegetables. Add the sliced onion and broccoli and cook, stirring until they are half cooked, about 10 minutes. Add the courgettes and continue cooking until nearly cooked, about another 5 minutes. Add the mangetout and continue stirring until heated through and changed colour before adding the spinach. Reduce heat, add the cornflour mixture and stir until the sauce has come to the boil and thickened. Serve with a chicken rice or quiche or add some cooked chicken or tofu before the sauce is added as a complete dish.

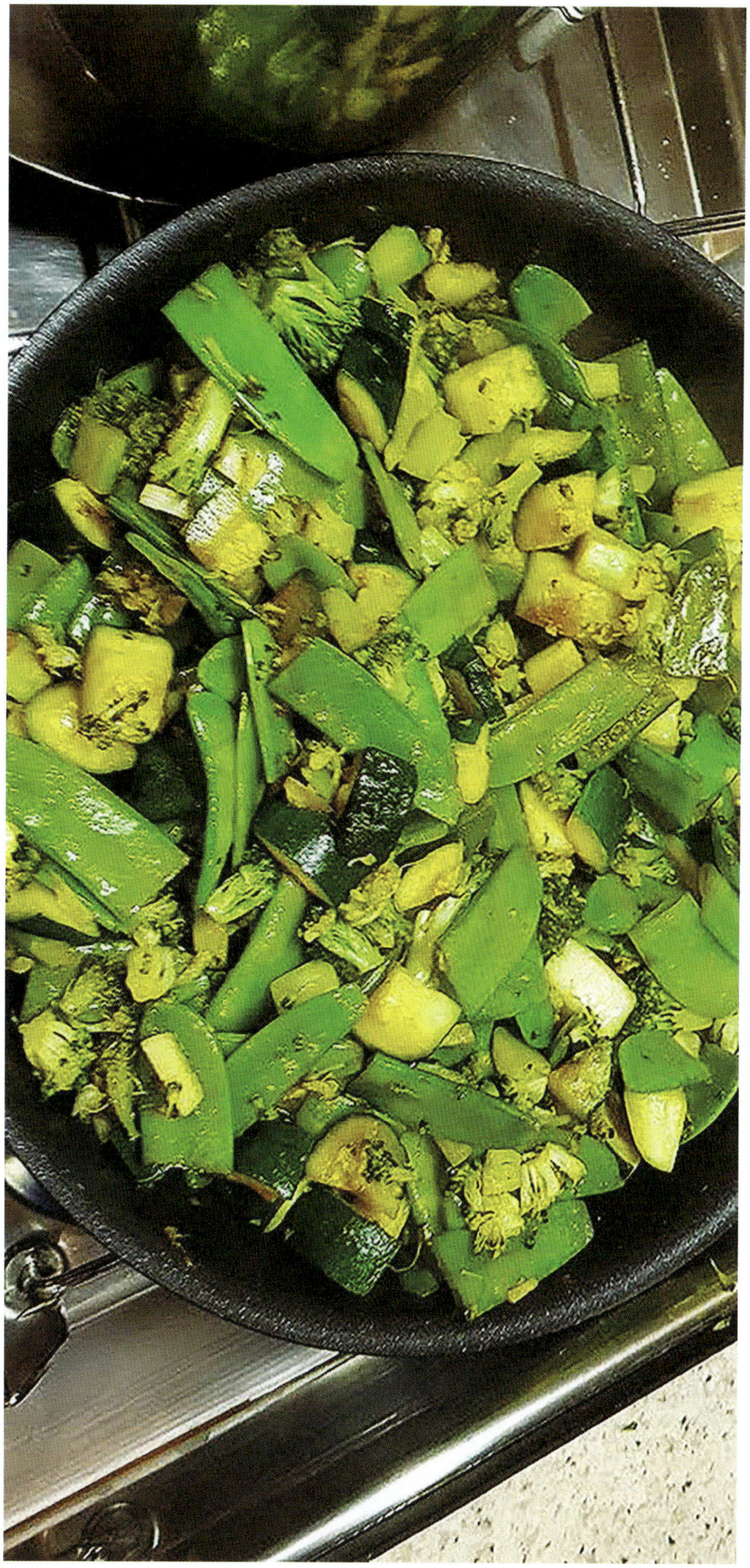

# Roasted Mediterranean Vegetables

Serves 4

Roasted Mediterranean vegetables make a quick versatile accompaniment to fish, meat or a vegetarian dish. Any left over vegetables can be eaten cold for lunch as a salad, used as a filling for a quiche or an omelette or reheated and served with a fried or poached egg as a light lunch or dinner.

*2 aubergine*
*3 peppers, green, red or yellow or a mixture sliced or 380 gms mini peppers*
*1kg new potatoes*
*2 courgettes*
*Olive oil*
*1 large onion*
*4 cloves of garlic*
*Salt and pepper*
*Sprigs of rosemary*

Cut the aubergine into cubes, slice the peppers. (You can leave the mini peppers whole.) Cut the small, new potatoes in half, slice the courgettes and onion. Mix together in a large roasting dish with sufficient olive oil to coat the vegetables, add salt and pepper to season. Peel the garlic and cut each clove in half. Add these to the vegetable mixture, cover with foil, and place in a hot oven 200°C, 180°C fan, Gas 6, for approximately an hour until the vegetables are cooked. Reduce the temperature after half an hour and remove the foil for the vegetables to colour. Serve with fish, meat, a fried egg or as an accompaniment.

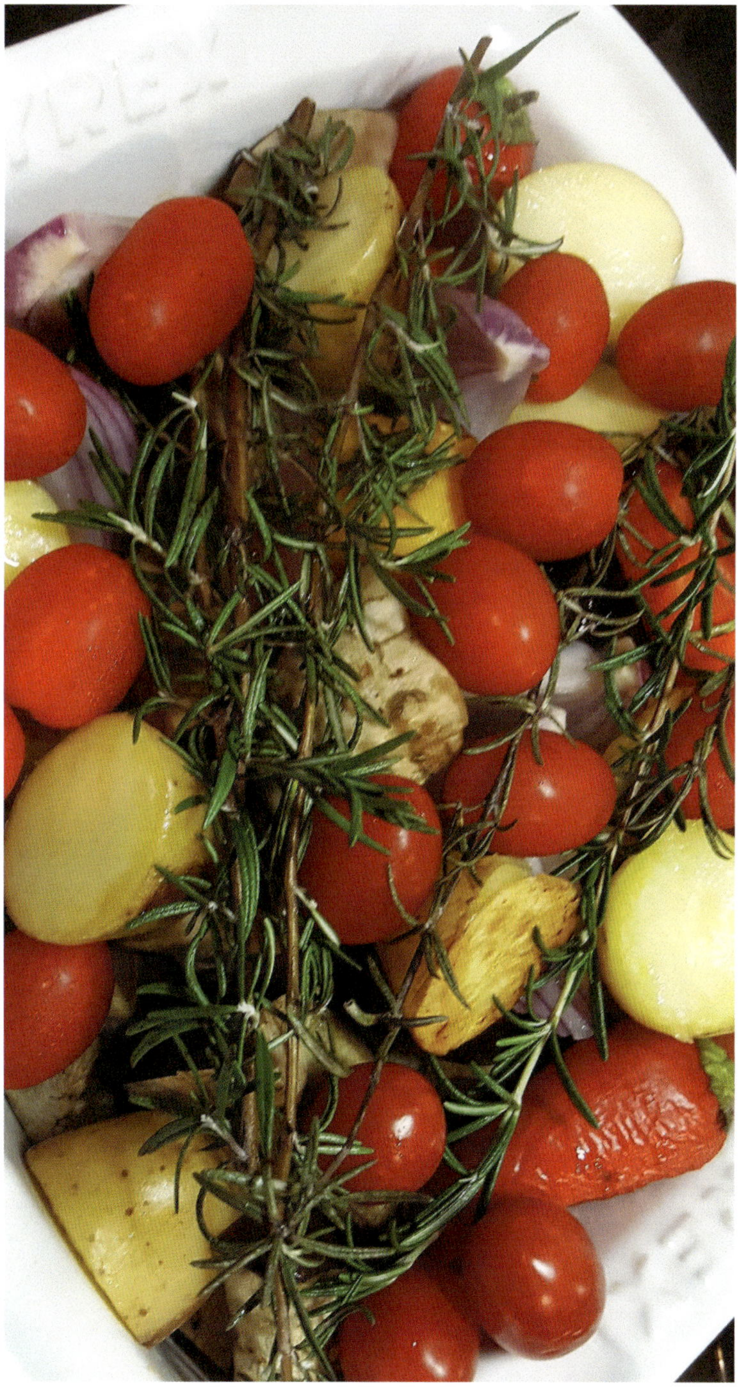

Sunset at Trebeurden, Brittany, North West France

# RYA TRAINING COURSE MEALS

These are the recipes that so many aspiring skippers requested and were promised after preparing and eating the dishes around the saloon table with fellow students. I hope you will enjoy preparing and eating them just as much on board your own yachts or at home and also enjoy the additional recipes in the book.

Safely tied up at dusk in Peel Harbour, Isle of Man

Peel Castle, Isle of Man

# Spanish Chicken with Peppers

Serves 4

I have found that there are times on board when slicing and chopping vegetables can be uncomfortable and time consuming. On RYA courses we get the crew around the saloon table to share the chore but using ready sliced peppers, for example, is an acceptable solution. If possible buy the chicken breasts already cut into chunks. I have included a jar of ready made sauce which makes the preparation easier but you can replace this with tinned chopped tomatoes and build up the flavour with bouillon and herbs.

*2 large onions*
*Olive oil*
*1 jar of Spanish chicken sauce (2 jars if you like a lot of sauce)*
*6 Chicken breasts cut into chunks*
*6 peppers (2 x green, 2 x red, 2 yellow)*
*4 Courgettes*
*2 cloves garlic crushed*
*3lb new potatoes*

Slice onions and peppers and fry gently in three tablespoons of olive oil in a large saucepan until the onion is transparent and the peppers softened. Add the garlic with the chicken and stir until the chicken changes colour. Add the jar of sauce and bring to the boil. Cover and simmer gently for 45 minutes or until the chicken is cooked. 20 minutes before the chicken is cooked add the sliced courgettes and continue simmering uncovered to reduce the sauce. Season to taste. Serve with new potatoes and a green salad.

### New Potatoes

Put the potatoes into a saucepan and just cover with water. Cover the pan with a lid and bring to the boil. Simmer gently for 15 to 20 minutes depending on size of potato. Drain and serve with the chicken.

### Variation

If you don't have a jar of Spanish chicken sauce add 2 tins of chopped tomatoes instead, a stock pot, a teaspoon of oregano, ground pepper and simmer gently until sauce has thickened and the chicken is cooked. Approximately 30 minutes. If there is left over sauce or for a vegetarian alternative add a tin of cannellini beans the next day and serve with steamed rice.

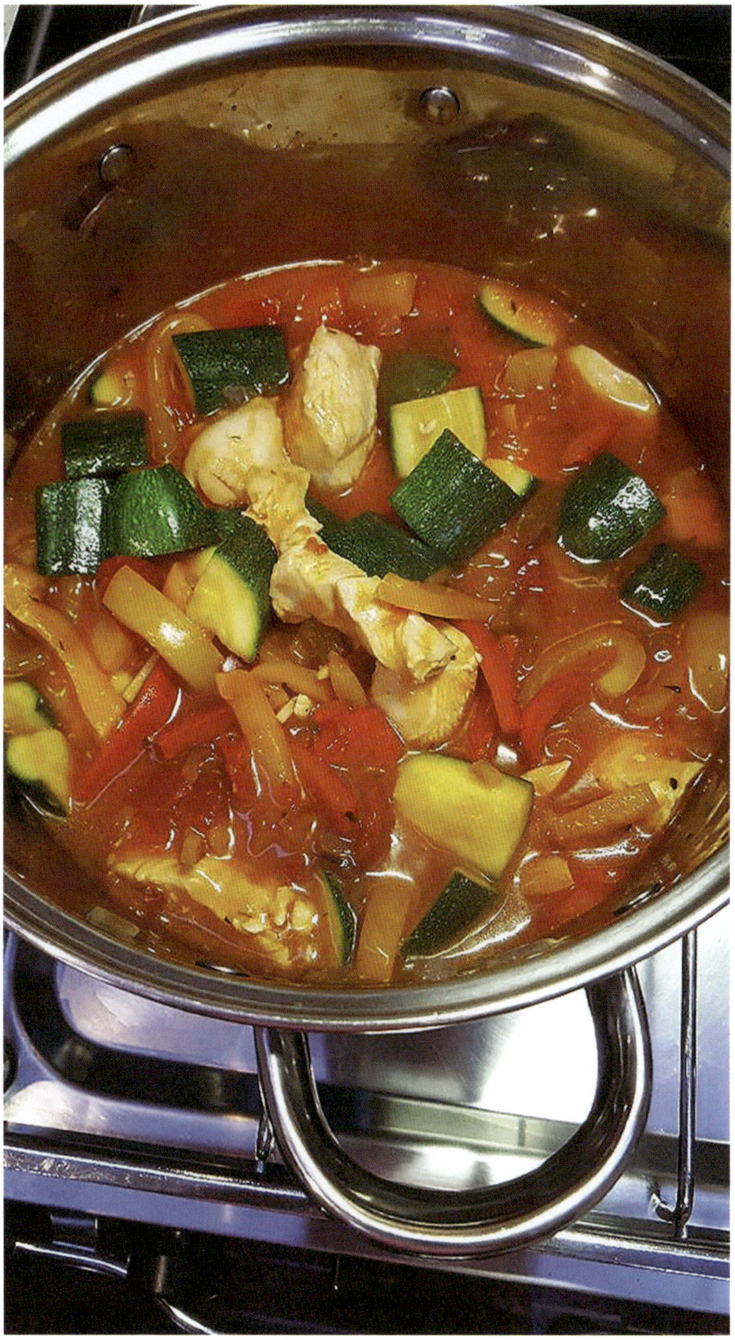

# Spanish Lentils

Serves 4

Lentil casserole has always been a favourite of mine and a good standby meal when there is little left on board and you arrive too late to go ashore and shop. The lentils can be cooking whilst you tie up. A vegetarian version with Spanish chorizo style sausages is equally good.

*500g green or Puy lentils*
*2 large onions, sliced*
*2 large carrots, sliced*
*2 sticks celery, sliced*
*4 small potatoes, sliced*
*1 green pepper, cubed*
*1 red pepper, cubed*
*2 cloves of garlic, crushed*
*2 tablespoons olive oil*
*1 tin of chopped tomatoes*
*2 tsps. of vegetarian bouillon*
*1 bay leaf*
*Mixed herbs*
*pepper*
*500g chorizo or vegetarian chorizo flavoured sausages (optional)*

Put the lentils in a large saucepan cover with water 5 cm above level of lentils and bring to the boil, reduce heat and simmer. Add the onions, carrots, peppers, garlic, celery, potatoes, bay leaf and a good pinch of mixed herbs with the tinned tomatoes and olive oil. Cook covered until the lentils and vegetables are tender. Simmer in total for approximately 40 minutes. Add more water if required. Add the skinned chorizo cut into chunks and continue cooking for a further 10-15 minutes. Season according to taste with the vegetarian bouillon. **The chorizo is quite salty so do not add salt until the end of cooking time when the lentils are tender and then according to taste.** Serve with couscous and steamed broccoli. If using vegetarian sausages put these in foil and place in a hot oven for approximately 15—20 minutes or fry in a non-stick pan .

**Couscous:** Put 1½ cups of couscous in a large bowl and just cover with boiling water, add a little olive oil. Stir, cover and set aside for 3 minutes. Serve with the lentils.

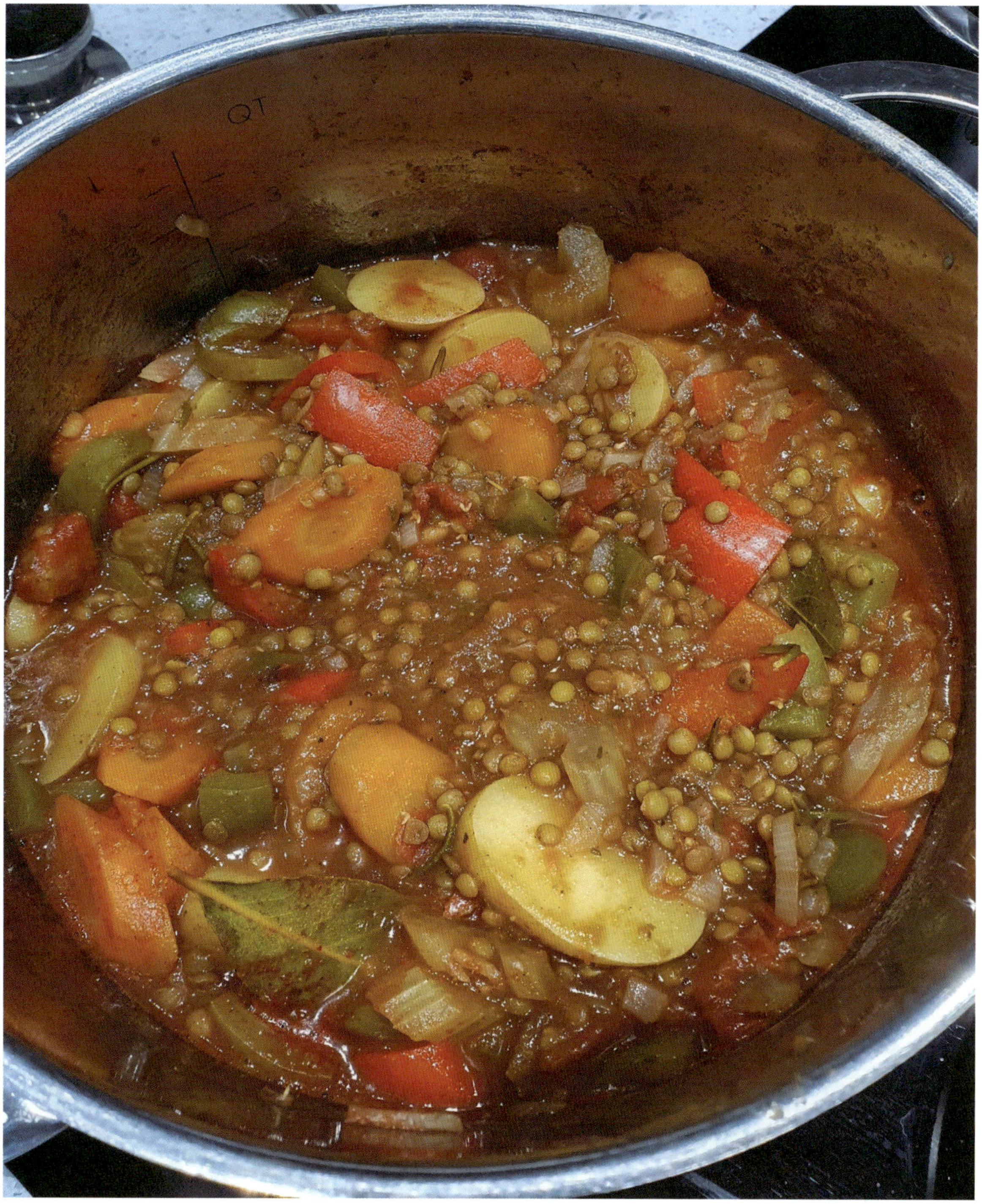

# Penne Bolognaise

## Serves 4

This is always a favourite and quick to prepare on board. I have chosen penne but other pasta shapes are equally suitable. If your provisioning cupboard doesn't run to minced meat you can substitute this with Quorn mince, soya TSP mince or lentils. If using lentils use 500 gms and reconstitute them. The sugar is added to balance the acidity of the tomatoes and you may need to adjust the amount of sugar according to taste.

*1kg minced meat*
*2 large onions chopped*
*2 large carrots, cut into cubes*
*1 yellow pepper, sliced*
*2 cloves of garlic , crushed*
*2 tin chopped tomatoes*
*2 tablespoons of tomato puree*
*1 teaspoon dried oregano*
*2 tsps. vegetarian bouillon*
*black pepper, salt, sugar*
*olive oil*
*grated cheese*
*500g penne pasta*

In a large saucepan heat 2 tablespoons of olive oil, add the minced beef, onion, carrots and garlic and cook until the meat has changed colour. Add the oregano, tinned tomatoes and tomato puree with the bouillon, a pinch of salt, freshly ground black pepper and approximately 1 teaspoon of sugar, bring to the boil and simmer gently for 40 minutes.

Meanwhile bring a large pan of water to the boil. 15 minutes before the sauce is ready cook the pasta by adding it to the boiling water and simmer gently until tender approximately 12 minutes. Drain. Serve the sauce with the pasta, grated cheese and garlic bread.

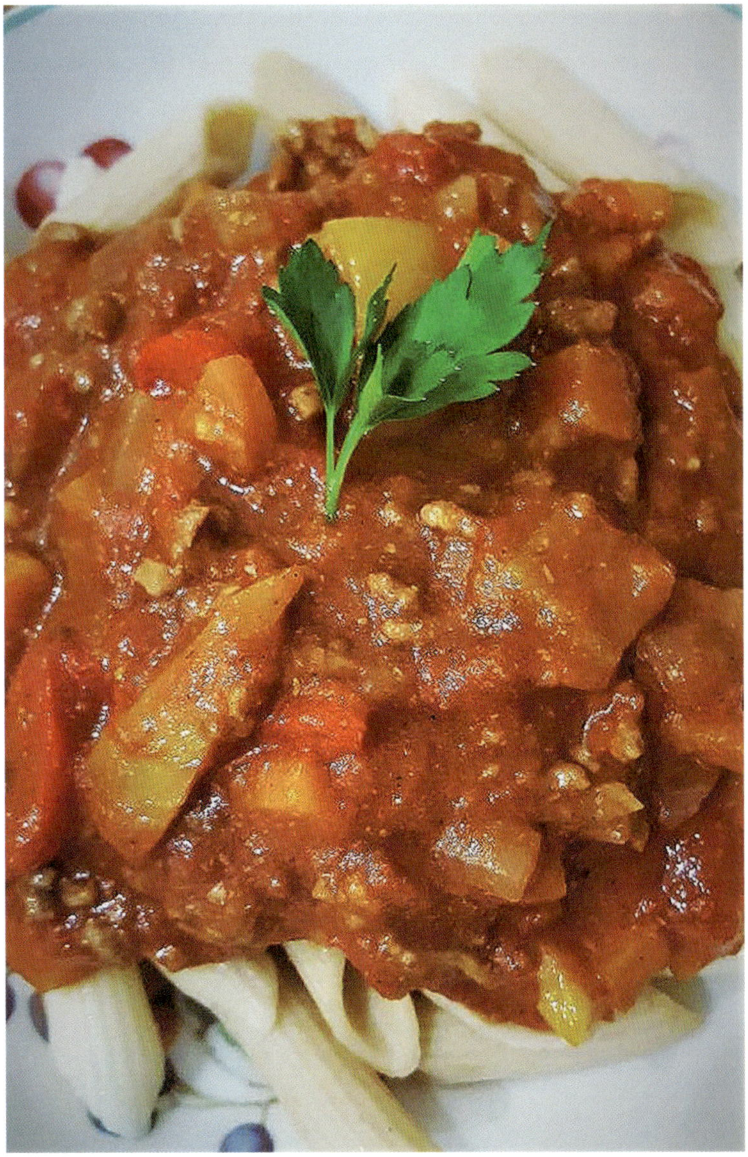

# Moroccan Lamb with Chilli and Ginger

Serves 4

Buy a cut of meat that only needs quick cooking unless you have a pressure cooker or are in harbour for a few days and long slow cooking is possible. This dish can also be vegan leaving the meat out altogether and replaced with TSP chunks although the chickpeas together with the couscous provide sufficient protein.

1 onion chopped
2 cloves of garlic, crushed
2 tins chickpeas, rinsed and drained
750g lean lamb, cubed
2 chillies chopped (optional)
2 tablespoons fresh ginger finely chopped or grated
2 tsp ground cumin
1 tin of tomatoes
1 jar of red wine sauce
2 tsp powdered vegetable bouillon
1 large aubergine cubed
2 tablespoons olive oil

Heat the oil in a large saucepan and add the meat and cubed aubergine, fry for 2 – 3 minutes. Turn down the heat and add the onion, cumin, ginger and garlic and stir through, cooking for a further 30 seconds. Add the tomatoes, the jar of sauce, bouillon and chickpeas and bring to the boil. Reduce the heat and simmer gently for 30 to 40 minutes or until the meat is tender. Serve with couscous.

## Couscous
Put 1½ cups of couscous in a large bowl and just cover with boiling water and add a little olive oil. Stir, cover and set aside for 3 minutes.

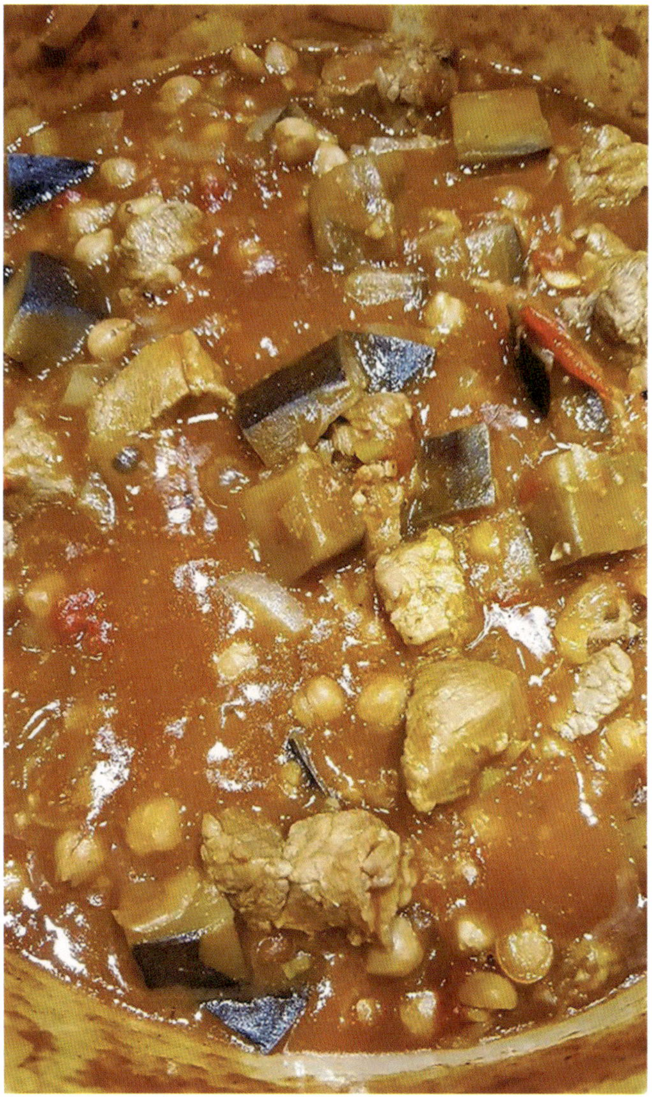

# Middle Eastern Tagine

Serves 4

This is a vegetarian dish using reconstituted textured soya protein which is an invaluable source of protein on board and can be used in most dishes as a substitute for meat. It can be purchased in chunks or as a mince substitute. It has little flavour but will take on the flavour of the spices and sauce in the dish.

*2 tins chick peas, rinsed and drained*
*1 onion, chopped*
*2 cloves garlic, crushed*
*150g Soya protein cubes reconstituted in vegetable stock*
*8 dried apricots, chopped*
*2 chillies chopped (optional)*
*2 tablespoons fresh ginger finely chopped or grated*
*2 tsp ground cumin*
*1 tsp ground turmeric*
*½ tsp ground cinnamon*
*1 tin of tomatoes*
*1 jar of red wine sauce*
*1 stockpot*
*1 large aubergine cubed*
*2 tablespoons olive oil*

Heat the oil in a large saucepan and add the onion and aubergine, fry for 2 – 3 minutes turn down the heat and add the cumin, turmeric, cinnamon with the ginger and garlic and stir through, cooking for a further 30 seconds. Add the tomatoes, the jar of sauce, the stockpot and the chickpeas together with the reconstituted soya protein and bring to the boil. Reduce the heat and simmer gently for 30 to 40 minutes or until the vegetables are cooked through and the soya protein is soft. Serve with couscous.

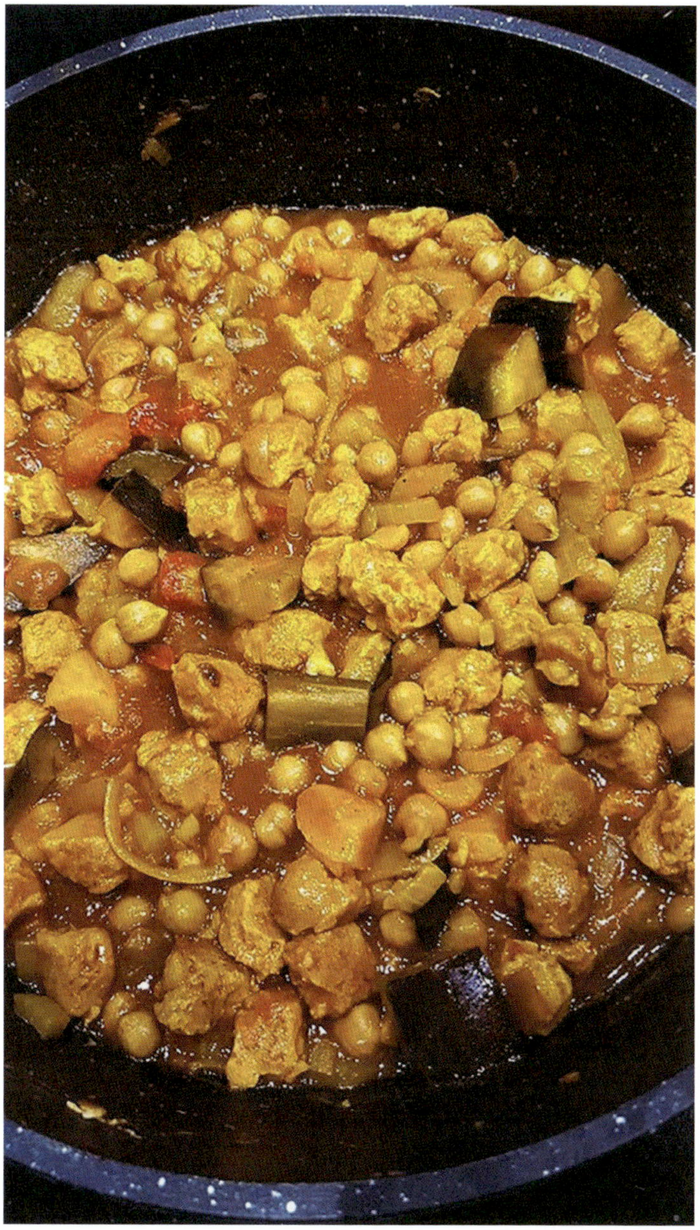

# Chilli con Carne

Serves 4-6

A firm favourite on board and can be made with textured soya protein, or Quorn mince if no meat is available. The guacamole, corn chips and grated cheese make this a special meal. More chilli can be added according to taste. To prevent the rice sticking use a diffuser mat. I have found if you take the covered rice off the heat once it has come to the boil it will continue to absorb water and you can put it back later to finish cooking. It also frees up a gas ring if needed.

*2 large onions*
*2 carrots*
*2 tins of kidney beans in chilli sauce*
*1kg lean minced beef*
*2 tins chopped tomatoes*
*2 peppers*
*2 cloves of garlic*
*2 tsps. ground cumin*
*Mixed herbs*
*Olive oil*
*Basmati rice*

Slice onions and peppers, finely slice carrots, crush garlic and fry gently together in three tablespoons of olive oil in a large saucepan until the onion is transparent and the peppers softened. Add the minced meat and stir until it changes colour. Add the tinned tomatoes, the kidney beans, the cumin and a pinch of mixed herbs and simmer for at least half an hour or until the sauce is reduced and thickened and the meat is tender. Season according to taste. Serve with rice, guacamole dip, grated cheese, tortilla chips and a salad made with salad leaves

**Perfect Rice:** Measure 2 cups of rice and place in a saucepan with four cups of water. Bring to the boil and cover, cook on a very low heat until all the water is absorbed and the rice is fluffy and cooked. This should take approximately 12 minutes.

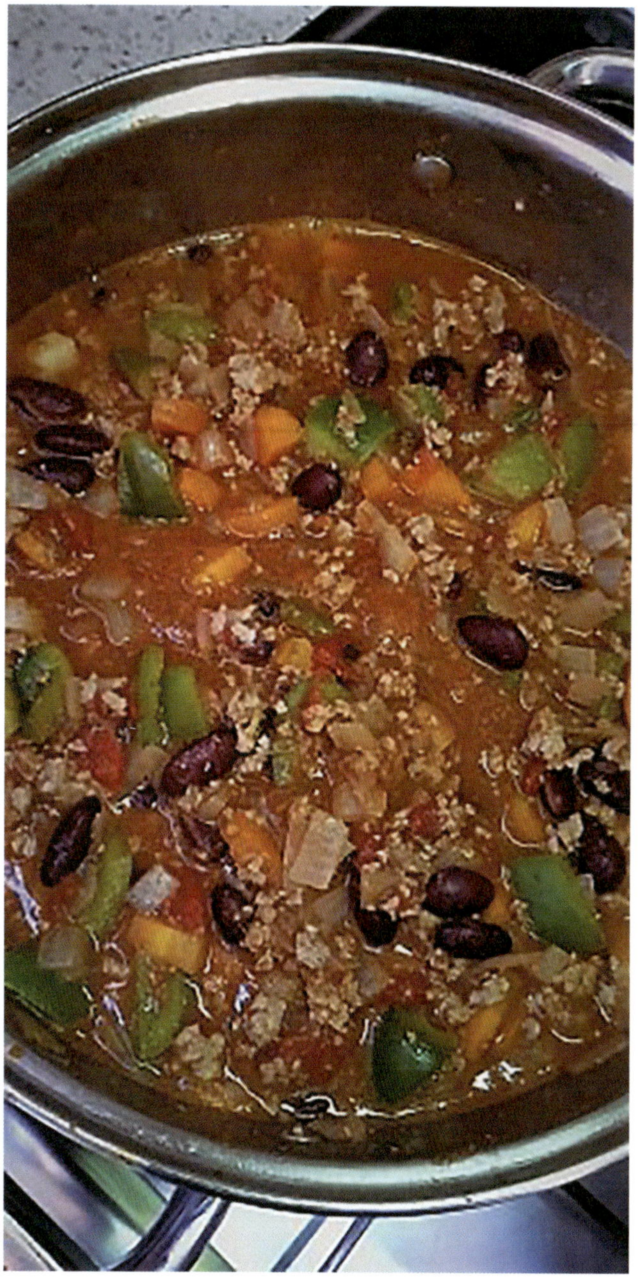

# Balti Curry

Serves 4-6

When provisioning it helps to buy turkey breast already cubed which reduces preparation time and any mess on board. If you like your curry hotter just add additional chilli. Everyone usually has there own preference for spiciness so put a bottle of chilli sauce or tabasco on the table when serving.

*1kg turkey meat, cubed*
*1 onion, sliced*
*3 medium tomatoes, chopped*
*2 carrots, sliced*
*1 large potato, cut into small cubes*
*2 jars of Balti Curry sauce*
*150g sugar snap peas*
*150g baby sweetcorn*
*Olive oil*
*4-6 small naan bread*
*Mango chutney*

In a large saucepan heat the olive oil, add the turkey cubes and stir over a moderate heat until the meat changes colour. Add the onion, carrots and potato. Cook for a few minutes. Add the chopped tomatoes and the Balti curry sauce and simmer gently, covered, for 25 – 30 minutes or until the turkey is tender. Add the baby sweetcorn 5 minutes before end of cooking time and the sugar snap peas 3 minutes before. Serve with rice, warmed naan bread and mango chutney.

**Perfect rice:** Measure 2½ cups of basmati rice and place in a saucepan with 5 cups of water. Bring to the boil, reduce the heat to a very gentle simmer, cover and cook until the water has been absorbed and the rice is fluffy and cooked. This should take approximately 12 minutes.

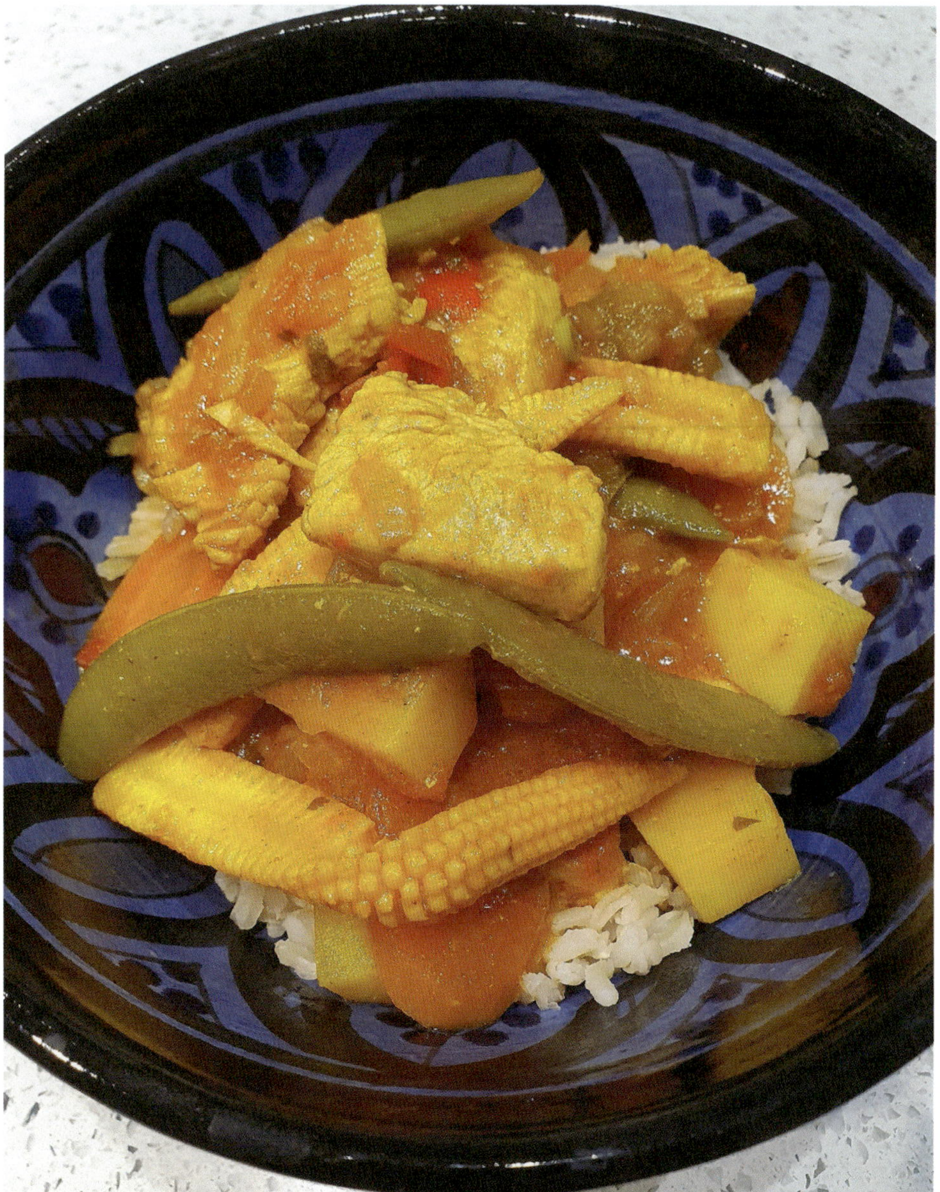

Safely over the bar at Salcombe en route to France

# Dinner

The evening meal, after a long day sailing, is something that we all look forward to where we can relax, dry off and glow after an exhilarating sail. I have split this section into two so that those aspiring competent crews, day skippers, coastal skippers and yachtmasters will recognise the dishes they prepared and ate whilst on board. (See RYA training course meals page 77)

Twilight, Peel Harbour, Isle of Man, when thoughts turn to the evening meal

# Merluza en Salsa Verde

Serves 4

The harbour at Audierne, Brittany is in the heart of the town and surrounded by restaurants, hotels, a salon de thé with its patisserie and a poissonnerie which sells freshly caught fish, restocked twice a day.  This recipe is suitable for any white fish cutlets and is reminiscent of the Basque dish my mother cooked, Merluza en Salsa Verde.

*1 onion, finely chopped*
*½ kg of cooked new potatoes, sliced*
*4 large hake  or cod steaks on the bone*
*2 large cloves of garlic, crushed*
*2 large cloves of garlic, sliced and lightly fried in olive oil*
*1½ tbsp flour*
*Stock made up from Bouillon powder*
*1 glass of white wine (optional)*
*Large bunch of parsley, washed and chopped*
*Olive oil*

Heat the oil in a deep frying pan or large saucepan and gently fry 2 sliced garlic cloves until golden brown.  Take care not to burn it as it will become bitter.  Remove from the pan and set aside.  Add the onion to the oil with the crushed garlic and cook until transparent and soft.  Mix in the flour with the cooked onions and garlic and place the fish steaks on top with the white wine and stock.  The fish should be nearly covered by the stock and wine. Bring to the boil gently, over a low heat, moving the pan all the time as the sauce thickens then add the cooked sliced potatoes. After 6 minutes turn the fish steaks and simmer gently for a further 5 - 6 minutes until the fish loses its translucence and turns white.  Lift the fish onto plates, add the chopped parsley to the pan, stir well and spoon over the fish steaks.  Sprinkle with the fried garlic.  Serve with a green salad, asparagus or steamed broccoli.

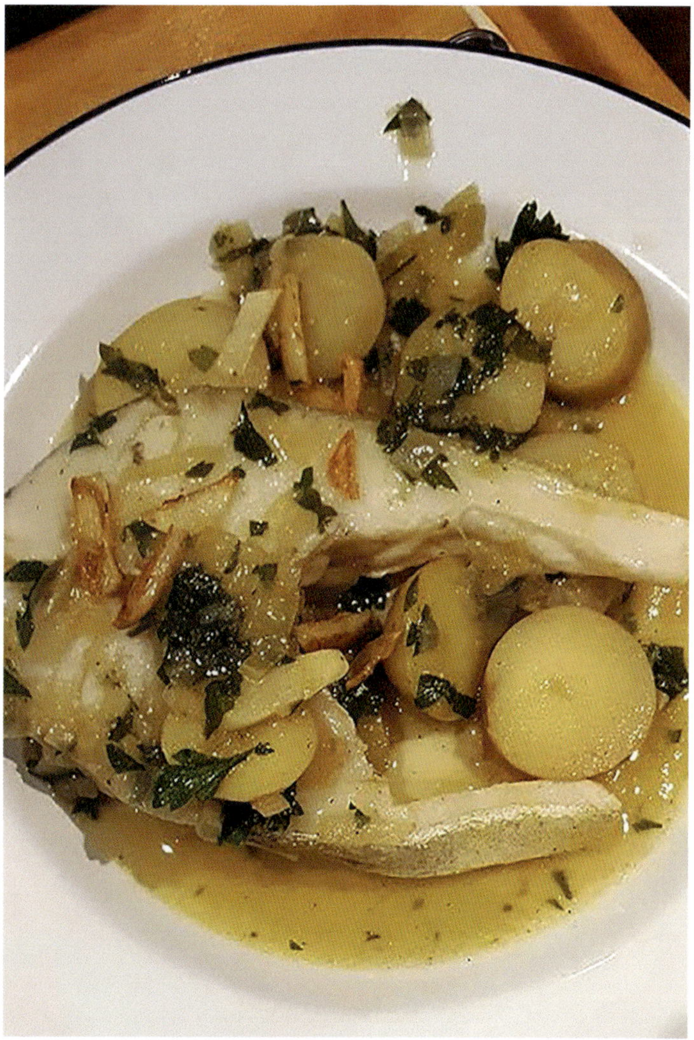

Nightfall in Audierne harbour

Audierne by day looking towards the patisserie and poissonnerie on the left

# Turkey Braised in Red Wine

Serves 4

In the meat counter at one of the supermarkets we visited on our journey down the west coast of France they sold turkey Osso Bucco which was turkey legs cut across the bone. You can ask a butcher to do this for you. It makes a lovely casserole and the marrow in the bone gives a richness to the sauce. I served it with new potatoes, steamed broccoli and roasted butternut squash. If steaming vegetables such as broccoli and only have two gas rings parboil the potatoes and place the steamer containing the vegetable on top of the potatoes and steam together so that they are all ready at the same time.

*1kg turkey Osso Bucco or turkey thigh meat cut into cubes*

*3 medium sized carrots, sliced*

*1 large onion, sliced*

*500g mushrooms, quartered*

*1 bottle of red wine*

*1 chicken stockpot*

*1 tsp dried rosemary*

*1 tsp dried thyme*

*Olive oil*

*Salt and pepper*

Heat the oil in a large saucepan and when hot but not smoking add the meat. Brown on each side. Take the meat out of the pan and put on a plate. Add the onion and carrot to the pan and soften in the oil and meat juices. Return the meat to the pan and pour enough wine to cover the meat and vegetables. Bring to the boil. Add the stockpot, the herbs and some pepper and simmer on a low heat for 45 minutes to 1 hour until the meat is tender. Check seasoning and adjust according to taste. 10 minutes before serving add the mushrooms. Serve with your chosen vegetables.

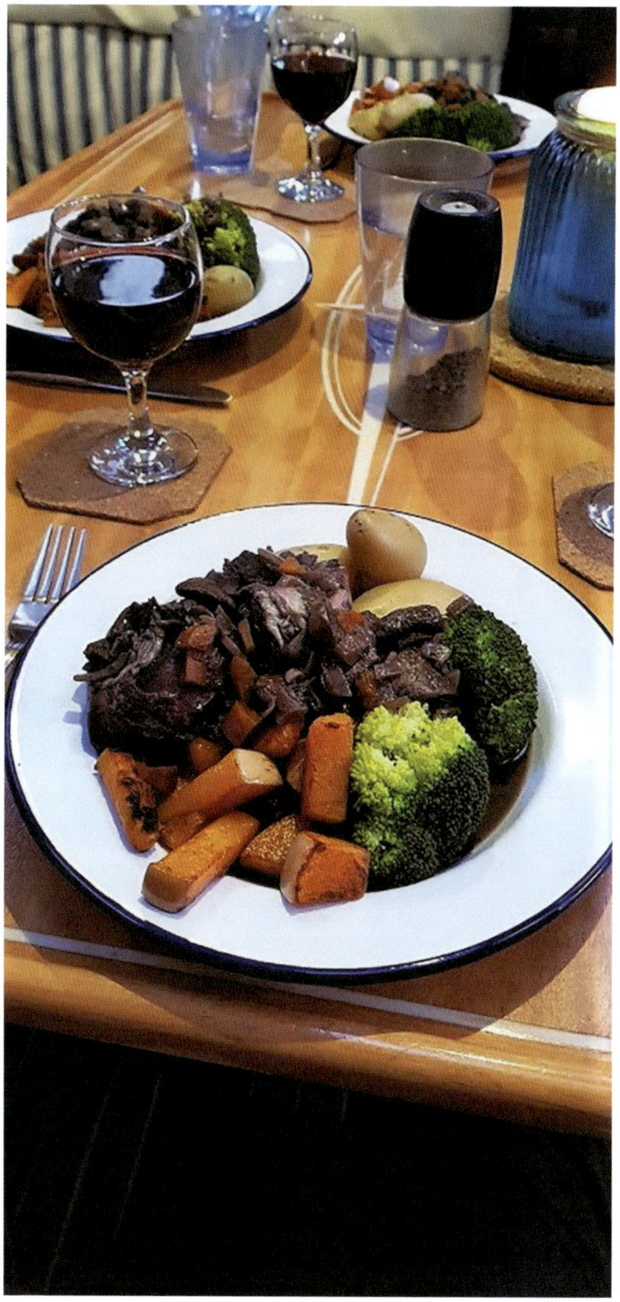

# Chicken Rice

Serves 4

A family favourite and a good way to use up cooked chicken. This recipe uses fresh chicken which is cooked before adding the vegetables and rice but it works equally well with cooked chicken off the bone. If using cooked chicken add it with the stock and remember if reheating cooked chicken do it only once. The recipe is a guide and other vegetables can be added to flavour the rice. I use wholemeal rice which takes longer to cook, approximately 25 minutes. Cook it according to the time recommended on the packet.

*1 large onion, chopped*
*2 cloves of garlic, crushed*
*2 carrots, cubed*
*4 tbsp olive oil*
*4 slices of ham, cubed*
*2 small chorizo, sliced*
*2 chicken breasts, cubed*
*6 chicken drumsticks*
*2 green peppers, cut into cubes*
*4 ripe tomatoes, roughly chopped*
*2 cups wholemeal paella (short grain) or risotto (Arborio) rice*
*2 chicken stock pots dissolved in 4 cups of water*
*1 tsp mixed herbs*
*Pepper*
*1 lemon*

Heat the oil in a large saucepan, add the chicken drumsticks and cubed chicken breasts and cook, covered slowly until nearly cooked, approximately 20 minutes. Add the onion, carrots, green pepper, chopped tomatoes and garlic and continue cooking over a low heat until they are soft. Add the rice and cook for 1 minute stirring all the time before adding the stock made up to 4 cups with water together with the herbs, pepper, ham and chorizo. Bring to the boil, taste the liquid to ensure it is well seasoned and cook on a very low heat, covered, for approximately 25 minutes or until the liquid is absorbed and the rice is cooked.

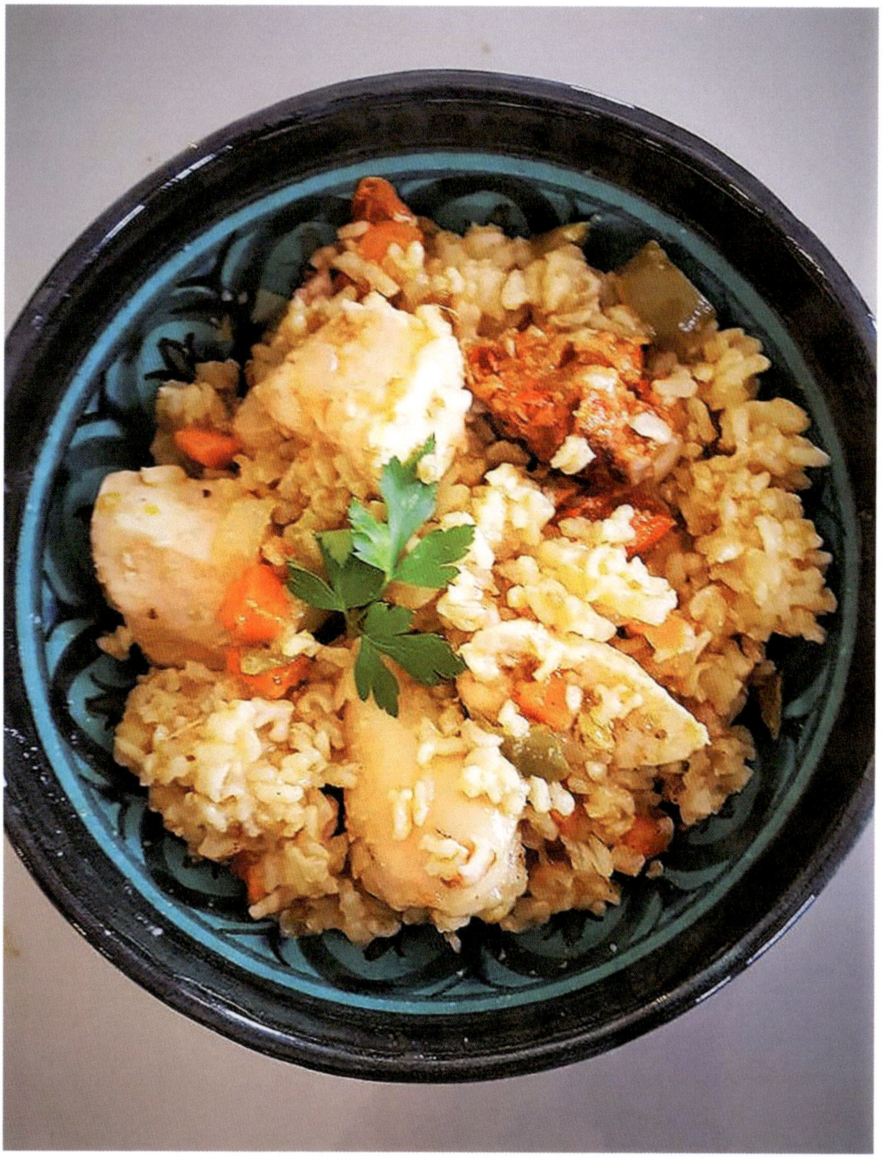

# Salmon Fillets with Puy Lentils

Serves 4

Inspired by Jamie Oliver, but a simplified version and perfect for cooking on board especially in areas where there is exceptionally fresh fish. It lends itself to any fresh fish fillets or a piece of chicken.

*500g Puy lentils*
*4 salmon or cod fillets with skin*
*4 tablespoons olive oil*
*Juice of 2 lemons*
*2 cloves of garlic crushed*
*2 good handfuls of mixed herbs, parsley, basil and mint chopped*
*1 bag of spinach*
*Salt and pepper*
*200ml natural yoghurt*
*3 tsp green pesto*

Put the lentils in a large saucepan, cover well with water, bring to the boil and simmer until tender, approximately 40 minutes. Drain the water from the lentils, return to the pan and season with pepper, salt, crushed garlic, lemon juice and 4 tablespoons of olive oil. Stir in the herbs and spinach until the spinach has wilted. Cover and keep warm.

Heat a tablespoon of olive oil in a frying pan and add the fish fillets skin side down and cook over a medium heat for a few minutes until the skin has browned. Turn the fillets over and cook for a further 3—5 minutes until just cooked. Mix the pesto into the yoghurt. Pile the lentils on plates place the fish on top and serve with pesto yoghurt, Mediterranean bread and a green salad.

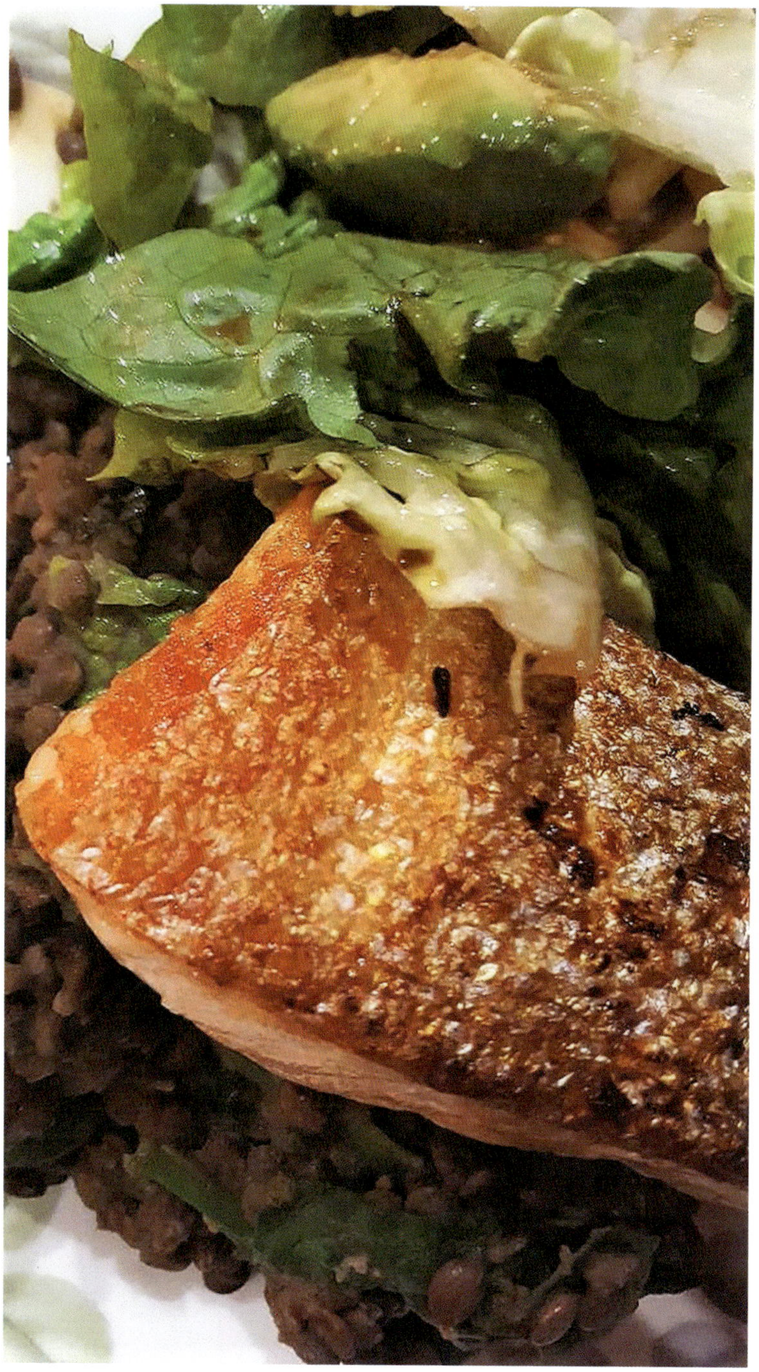

# Linguine Carbonara

Serves 4

This recipe always reminds me of my son coming home famished from work and needing something delicious and quick to make.  We have cooked together ever since he and my daughter could stand on a chair next to me and help.  So much fun.  They have both become wonderful, adventurous cooks and have each developed their own unique styles.

*227g linguine*
*3 tbsp olive oil*
*1 onion, finely chopped*
*113g chopped bacon or cooked ham*
*4 eggs*
*Salt and pepper*
*57g mature cheddar or parmesan cheese*

My son, talented and creative

Cook the linguine in a large saucepan of boiling water until tender.  Drain and rinse with cold water.  Leave to drain.  In the same saucepan heat the oil, add the onion and cook until transparent.  Add the ham or bacon and cook gently for 3 minutes. Add the drained pasta and toss lightly to mix. Beat four eggs in a bowl with a little salt and pepper.   Pour the eggs over the pasta and stir gently over low heat until the eggs begin to thicken.  Stir in the cheese and serve immediately with a green salad and garlic bread.

As a variation if you prefer not to eat ham or bacon, quickly fried mushrooms are equally delicious.  Use 8-10 mushrooms instead of the bacon.

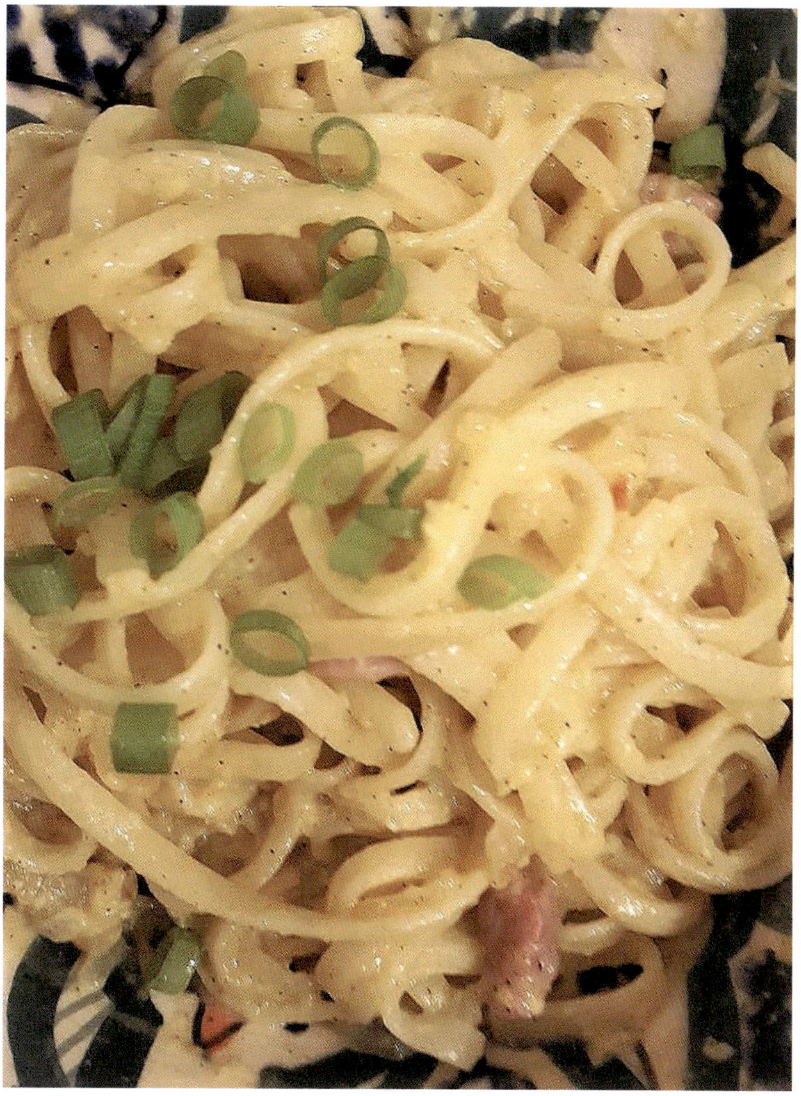

# Vegetarian Mince

*Serves 4*

A versatile mixture that can be served with pasta or rice and makes an excellent filling for a cottage pie, stuffing for peppers or a filling for a quiche with cheese sprinkled on the top.

*1 large onion, chopped*
*1 stick celery, sliced*
*2 carrots, chopped*
*Olive oil*
*3 cloves of garlic, crushed*
*6 mushrooms, chopped*
*1 green pepper, chopped*
*2 tins of chopped tomatoes*
*1 tbsp tomato puree*
*½ cup red lentils*
*1 cup of fine textured soya protein*
*2 tsp ground cumin*
*2 tsp ground coriander*
*1 tsp sugar*
*2 vegetable stock pot*
*2 tsp Marmite*
*1 tsp mixed herbs*
*black pepper*

Soften the onion in olive oil, in a large saucepan, until transparent, add the carrots, celery, mushrooms, green pepper and garlic and cook for 2 minutes. Add the rest of the ingredients with 3 cups of water and bring to the boil. Simmer gently for 30 minutes or until the sauce is reduced. Check seasoning and season to taste. Serve with any pasta, Parmesan cheese and a green salad.

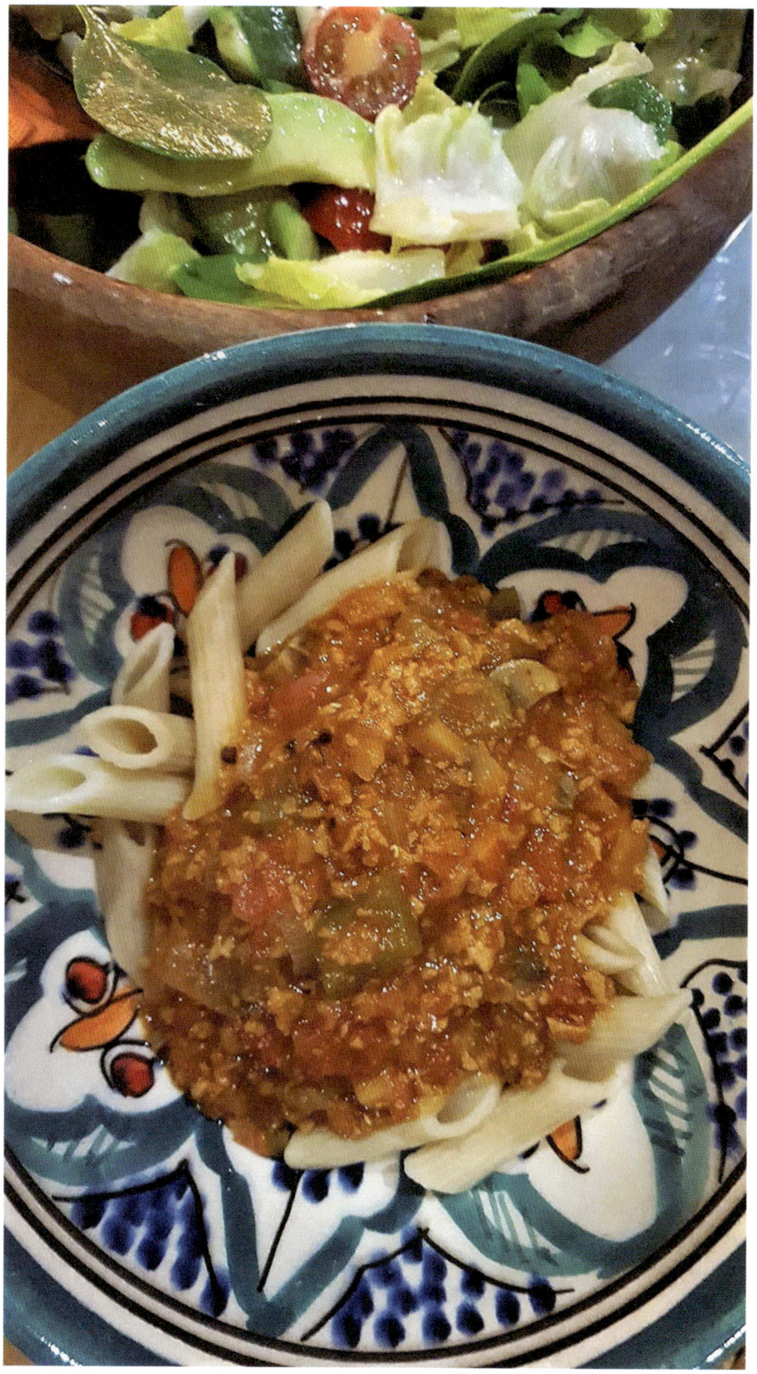

# Vegetable Chilli
Serves 4

This chilli can be made with the vegetables you have on board and the recipe is a guide. It is a great way to use up vegetables before buying fresh provisions. Delicious served with wholemeal rice, guacamole, tortilla chips, a salad and some grated cheese. The amount of chilli powder is added according to taste and a bottle of chilli sauce is essential if catering for varied tastes.

*1 large onion, chopped*
*Olive oil*
*3 cloves of garlic, crushed*
*¼ butternut squash, cubed*
*60g mushrooms, quartered*
*1 green pepper, sliced*
*2 courgettes, cubed*
*1 aubergine, cubed*
*2 tsps chilli powder*
*2 tsps ground cumin*
*2 tsps ground coriander*
*2 tsps turmeric*
*2 tins of chopped tomatoes*
*1 tbsp tomato puree*
*2 tins kidney beans in water*
*1 stock pot dissolved in 1 cup boiling water*
*2 tsp Marmite*
*1 tsp oregano*

In a large saucepan soften the onion in olive oil until transparent. Add the butternut squash, green pepper, courgettes, aubergine, mushrooms, chilli powder and garlic and cook for 2 minutes. Add the rest of the ingredients and bring to the boil. Simmer gently for 30 minutes or until the sauce is well reduced. Check seasoning and adjust according to taste. Serve with Perfect Rice (page 88).

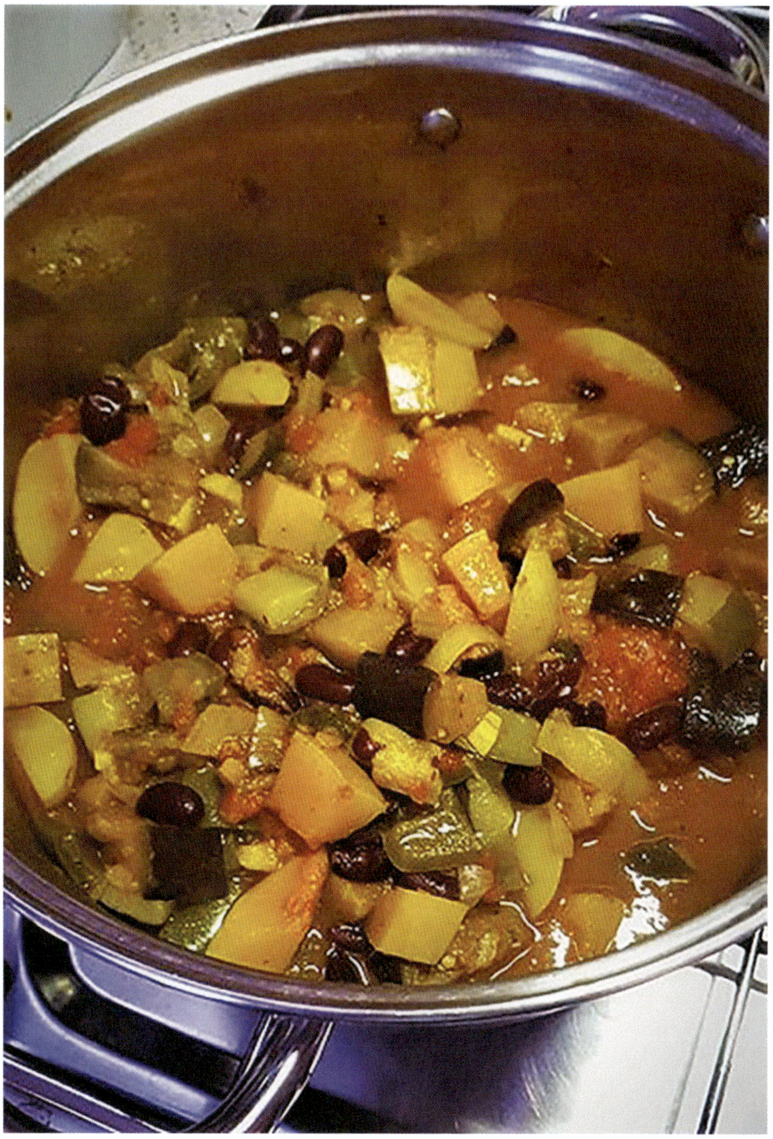

# Chicken with Noodles

Serves 4

This is a quick dish to prepare as the chicken is cooked. Taking the meat off the bone is the time consuming and messy part of this recipe so give yourself 10—15 minutes or so to get the meat ready.

*1 cooked roast chicken*

*3 tbsp olive oil*

*4 large ripe tomatoes*

*1 onion, chopped*

*2 sticks of celery, chopped*

*1 clove of garlic, crushed*

*A small piece of chopped fresh ginger*

*1 tsp dried oregano*

*1 bag washed spinach*

*227g noodles*

*1 stockpot*

*Vegetable bouillon*

*118 ml water*

*Pepper*

Take the meat off the cooked chicken and leave in chunks removing all skin and bones. Heat the olive oil in a large saucepan and add the onion, celery and garlic. Cook over a low heat until transparent. Add the chopped tomatoes, water, stockpot, oregano and the cooked chicken and simmer over a low heat for 10 minutes until the onion is cooked and the chicken heated through. Sprinkle 2 teaspoons of vegetable bouillon over the chicken mixture and mix in well. While the chicken mixture is simmering cook the noodles according to packet instructions. Add the spinach to the chicken mixture and stir through until the spinach has wilted. Finally add the cooked noodles and mix in well. Serve immediately.

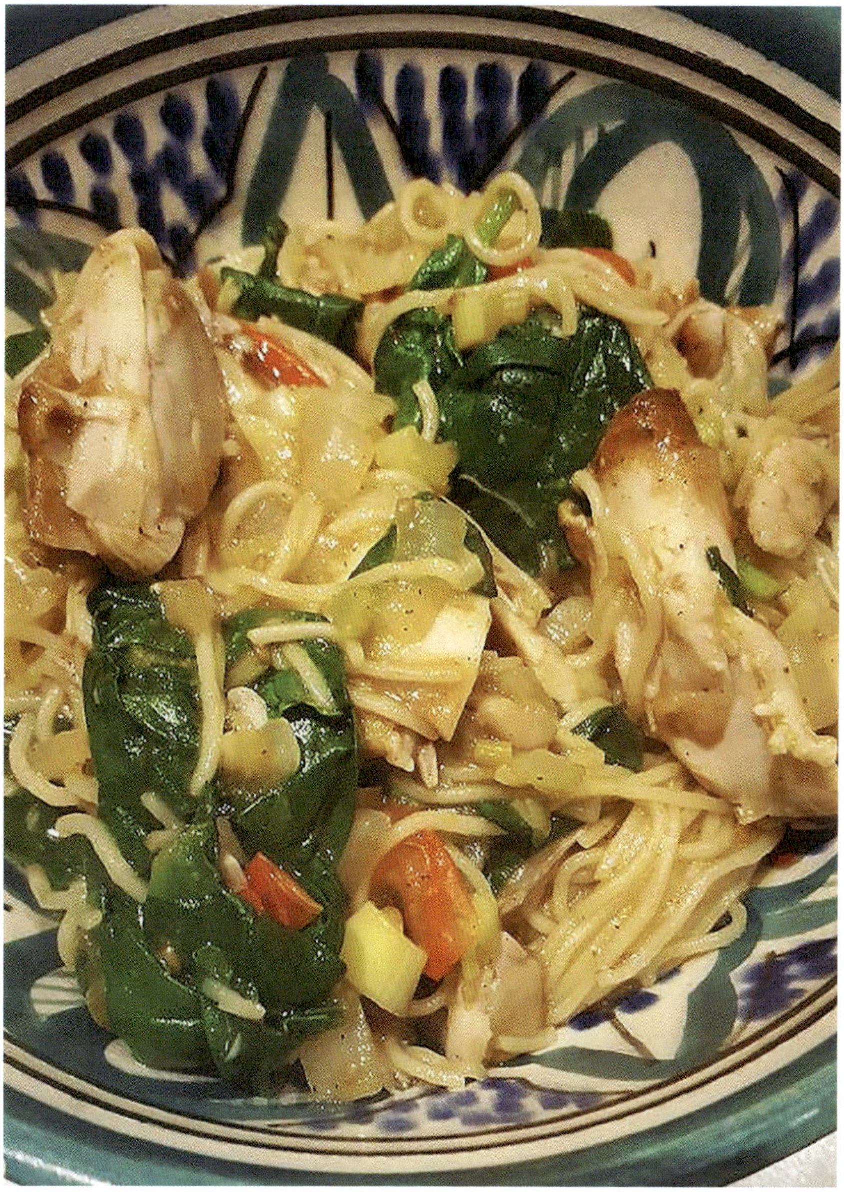

# Laksa

Serves 4

This is a dish that embodies the essence of Malaysia and takes me back to the Malacca straits sailing from Singapore to Penang. Simple to prepare on board and eaten out of a large bowl. I have used an already roasted chicken which are available at supermarkets. Alternately you could use fresh cubed fish fillets or prawns added instead of the chicken . They don't take more than a few minutes to cook through in the soup before adding the noodles.

1 roasted chicken
1 pack of fine rice noodles, enough for 4
4-5 oz fresh red chillies
1 small onion chopped
1 tablespoon ground turmeric
3 cm piece fresh ginger, peeled and finely chopped
2 tbsp olive oil
1½ litres stock made with 3 chicken stockpots or cubes
Mint and basil leaves, chopped
1 teaspoon tamarind paste
1 lemongrass stalk
Salt and pepper
1 pack mange tout and baby sweetcorn
6 chestnut mushrooms, sliced

*Garnish*
1 finely chopped chilli
A handful of mint finely chopped
1 lime

Remove the meat from the chicken and shred. In a large saucepan fry the chillies, small onion, turmeric and ginger in olive oil. When softened and transparent add stock, tamarind, lemongrass, mint and basil. Add the mangetout sliced lengthways, baby sweetcorn and chestnut mushrooms to the stock and simmer gently for 3 minutes. Add the shredded chicken to the hot chicken stock and heat through while you prepare the rice noodles according to the instructions on the packet. Just before serving add the juice of a lime to the stock and check seasoning. Put a serving of noodles at the bottom of a deep bowl. Ladle the chicken broth over the noodles and sprinkle with chopped chillies and mint.

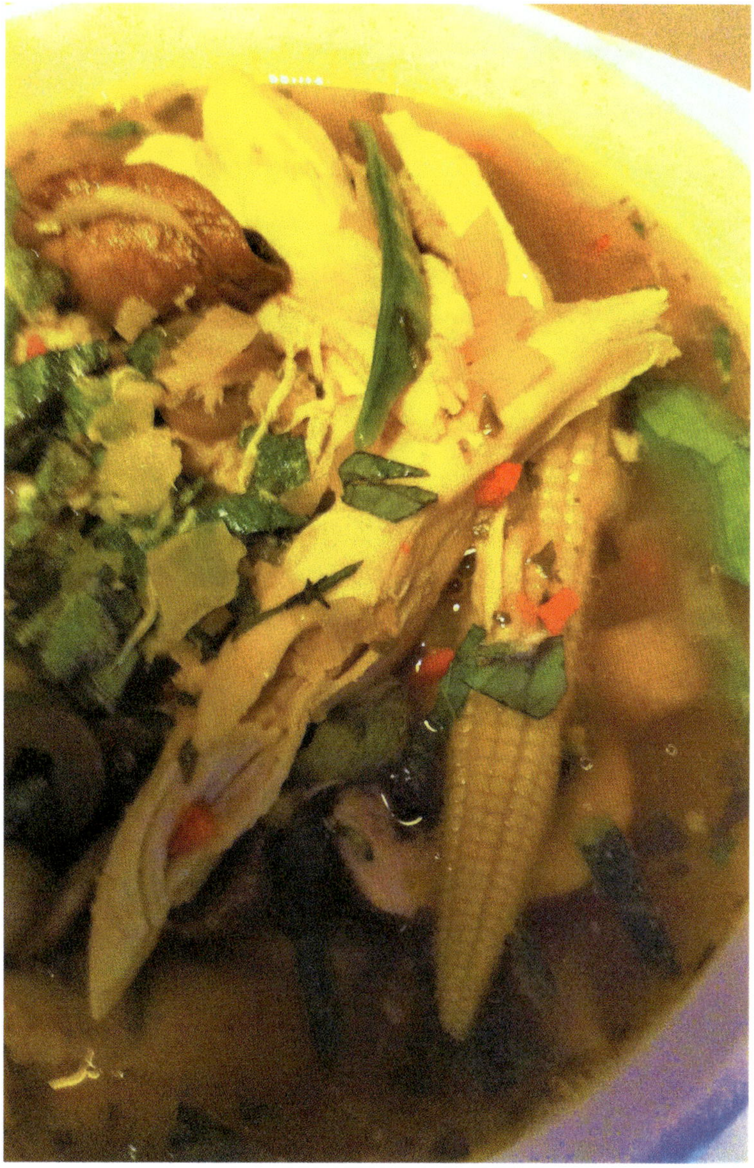

# Stuffed Peppers Braised in Tomato Sauce

Serves 4

Peppers can be stuffed with a variety of fillings and is an excellent way of using up left overs. The stuffing can be vegetarian, rice with pine nuts, or with minced meat. Slow cooking in a tomato sauce concentrates the flavour of the sauce and creates a meal in itself served with a green salad and bread.

*4 Large peppers, green, red or yellow with the lid removed and deseeded*
*1 large onion, chopped*
*2 cloves of garlic*
*2 carrots, thinly sliced*
*4 tablespoons olive oil*
*2 cups rice*
*1 cup of pine nuts*
*2 stock pots dissolved in 4 cups of water*
*1 tsp mixed herbs*
*Pepper*
*1 lemon*

Heat the oil in a medium saucepan and soften the onion, carrots, and garlic over a low heat. Add the rice, cook for 1 minute stirring all the time. Add the stock the herbs and pepper. Bring to the boil, cook on a low heat, covered, for approximately 15 minutes or until the liquid is absorbed and rice is cooked. Stir in pine nuts and stuff peppers with the rice mixture.

## Tomato sauce
*1 large onion, chopped*
*2 cloves of garlic*
*2 tablespoons of olive oil*
*2 tins chopped tomatoes or passata*
*1 teaspoon mixed herbs*
*Pinch sugar*
*Salt and pepper to taste*

Prepare tomato sauce in large saucepan while rice is cooking. Heat olive oil in the saucepan add onion and soften. Add finely chopped garlic, herbs, chopped tomatoes and sugar. Bring to the boil and simmer gently. Place the stuffed peppers upright in the tomato sauce wedged together to provide support so they don't slide into the sauce. Put the pepper lids on top of each, cover saucepan and simmer for 30-40 minutes or until the peppers are cooked.

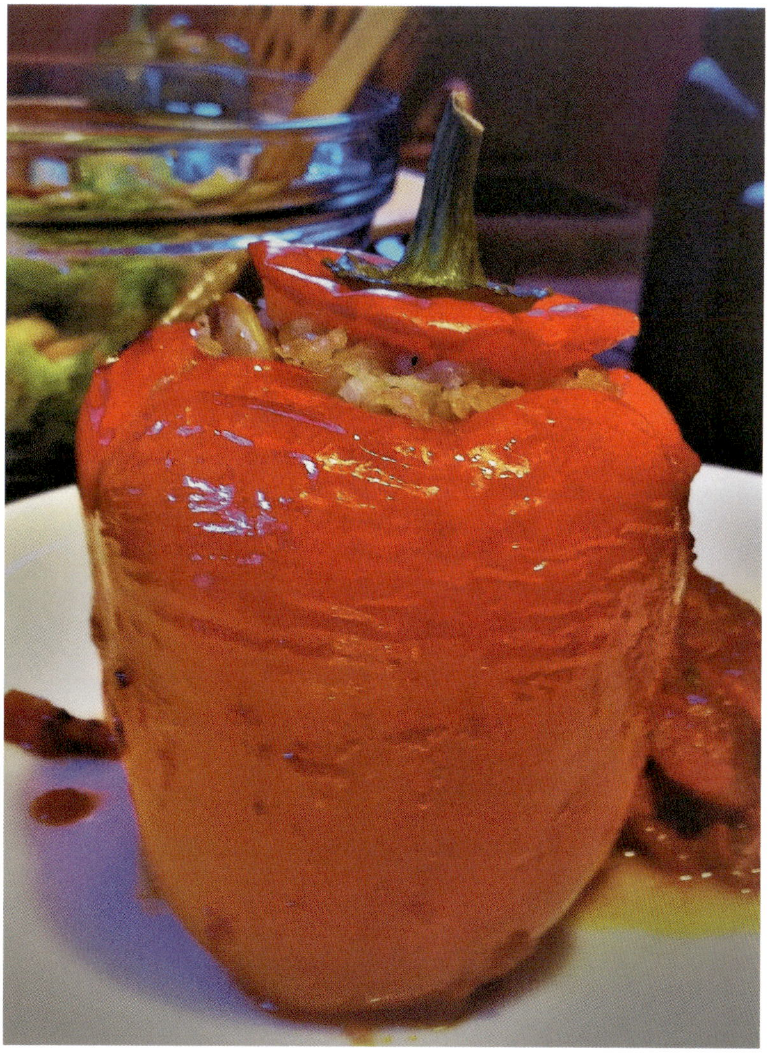

# Armenian Lamb

## Serves 4

This dish takes me back to the Brisbane river when I lived on board a trimaran at the botanical garden moorings. The first part of my journey to work was rowing the dinghy and tying up on the ferry jetty before taking a bus for the rest of the journey. I invited some of my work colleagues for dinner aboard one evening and this was on the menu served with a pistachio pilaf and fresh peaches in white wine for dessert. It is equally as good made with chicken or turkey.

*1kg cubed, lean lamb*
*1 tbsp olive oil*
*28g butter*
*2 medium sized onions, chopped*
*1 aubergine, cubed*
*2 cloves of garlic*
*1 tablespoon ground cumin*
*2 tablespoons ground allspice*
*1 tablespoon tomato puree*
*1 tin of chopped tomatoes*
*½ litre stock*
*Salt and pepper*

Heat the oil in a large saucepan and when warm add the butter together with the cubed lamb. Cook over a medium heat until it is slightly browned. Add the onions and cook gently until the onion becomes opaque. Add the garlic, cumin, allspice, tomato puree and mix well. Pour in the stock and tinned tomatoes and cover. Simmer gently until the lamb is tender and the sauce has thickened. Serve with Pistachio Pilaf (page 118).

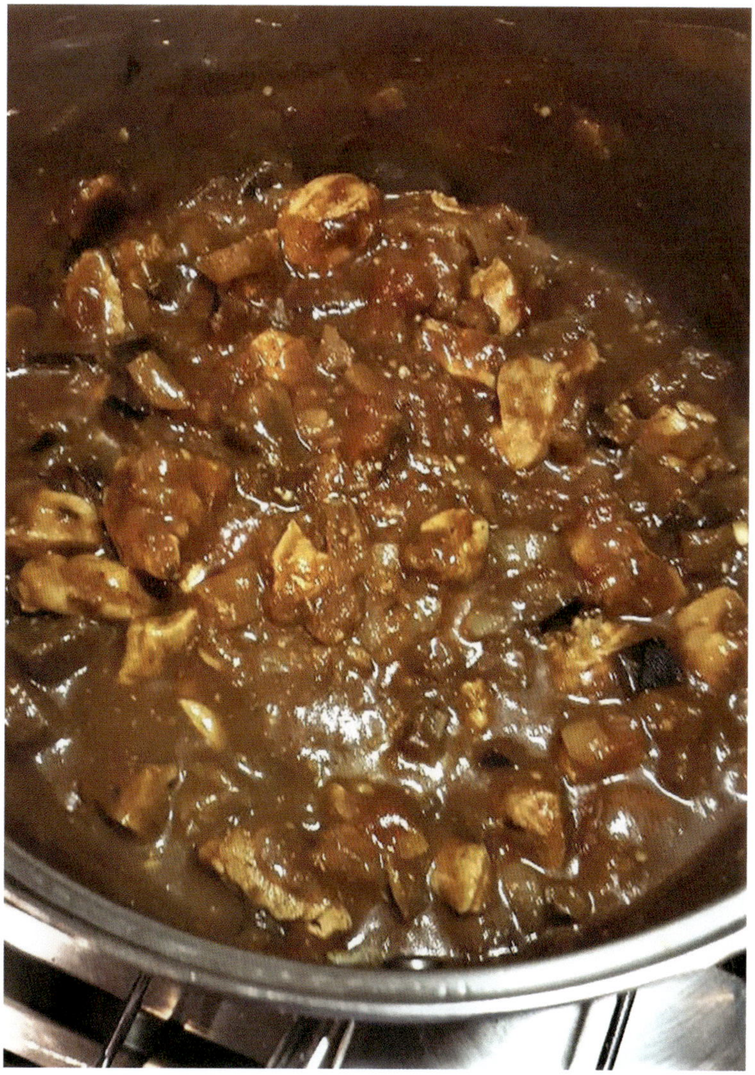

# Pistachio Pilaf

Serves 4

*2 tablespoons olive oil*

*1 small onion, finely chopped*

*225g basmati rice*

*425 ml stock*

*Salt and pepper*

*85g currants*

*85g shelled pistachio nuts chopped*

Warm the oil in a medium saucepan add the onion and cook on a low heat until just turning colour. Add the rice and cook gently for 2 minutes. Pour on the stock and add the seasoning. Simmer gently, covered until the rice is cooked and stock absorbed. Approximately 12-15 minutes. Fork through the currents and nuts before serving.

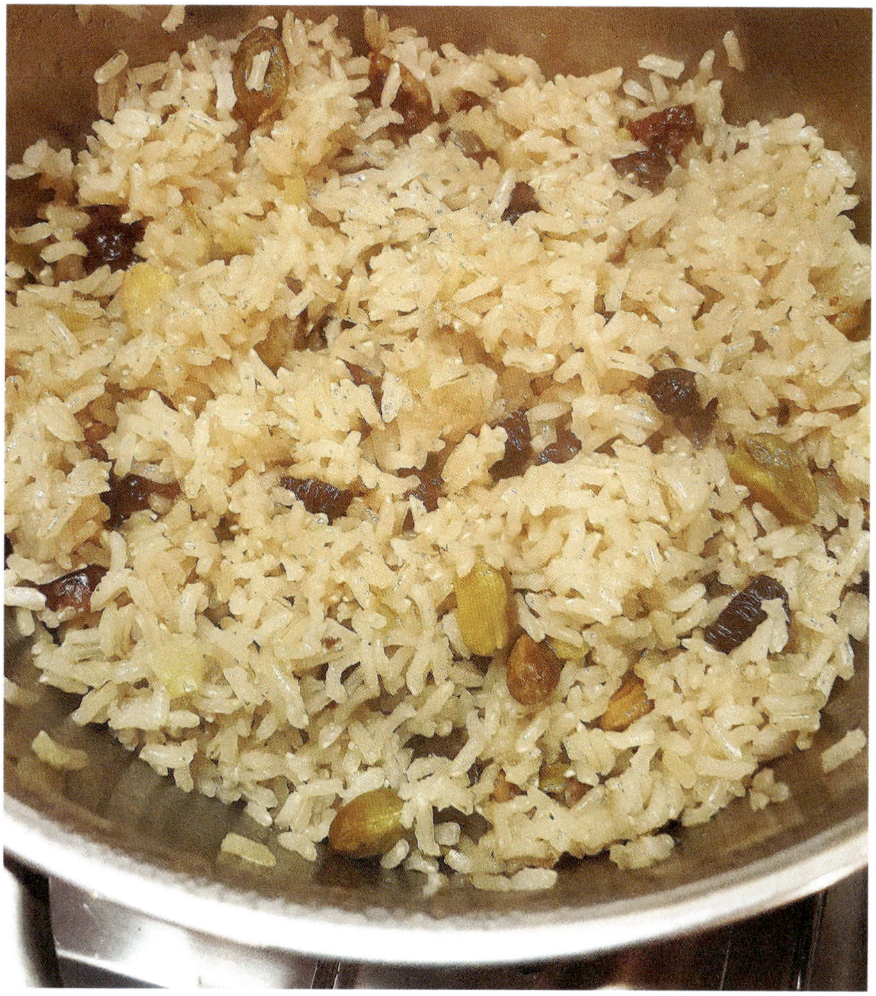

# Malaysian Satay Un-Skewered

Serves 4

This recipe is a classic satay but yachts don't usually have a grill so the marinated chicken is cooked in a non-stick frying pan in a little oil or baked in the oven. Use a baking tray with sides so that the juice from the meat doesn't drip over the edges into the oven. Lining your baking tray with waxed paper prevents laborious washing up. If you have a barbecue the meat can be threaded onto skewers and cooked over a moderate heat. An easy but impressive dish to prepare if you have invited guests on board. For vegans this can be made with sliced tofu.

1kg chicken breasts or pork fillet, cubed

## Marinade
*1 large onion, finely chopped*
*3 garlic cloves creamed to a paste with a little salt*
*1 ½ teaspoons of ground pepper*
*2 teaspoons ground cumin*
*1 tablespoon ground coriander*
*3 cm piece of root ginger, grated*
*1 teaspoon ground turmeric*
*Juice of one lemon*
*Juice of one lime*
*2 tablespoons olive oil*

Mix all the marinade ingredients together and add the cubed meat. Marinade for 15—30 minutes. Line a baking tray with foil or greaseproof paper and lightly oil. Put the marinated chicken pieces on the tray, cover with foil and bake in a hot oven 190°C, 170°C fan, Gas 5, until browned and cooked through, approximately 20 - 25 minutes. The meat should be firm and have changed colour but check by taking a piece out, the flesh should be white. Remove the foil for the last 5 minutes of cooking. Meanwhile prepare the sauce.

Sauce recipe continued overleaf

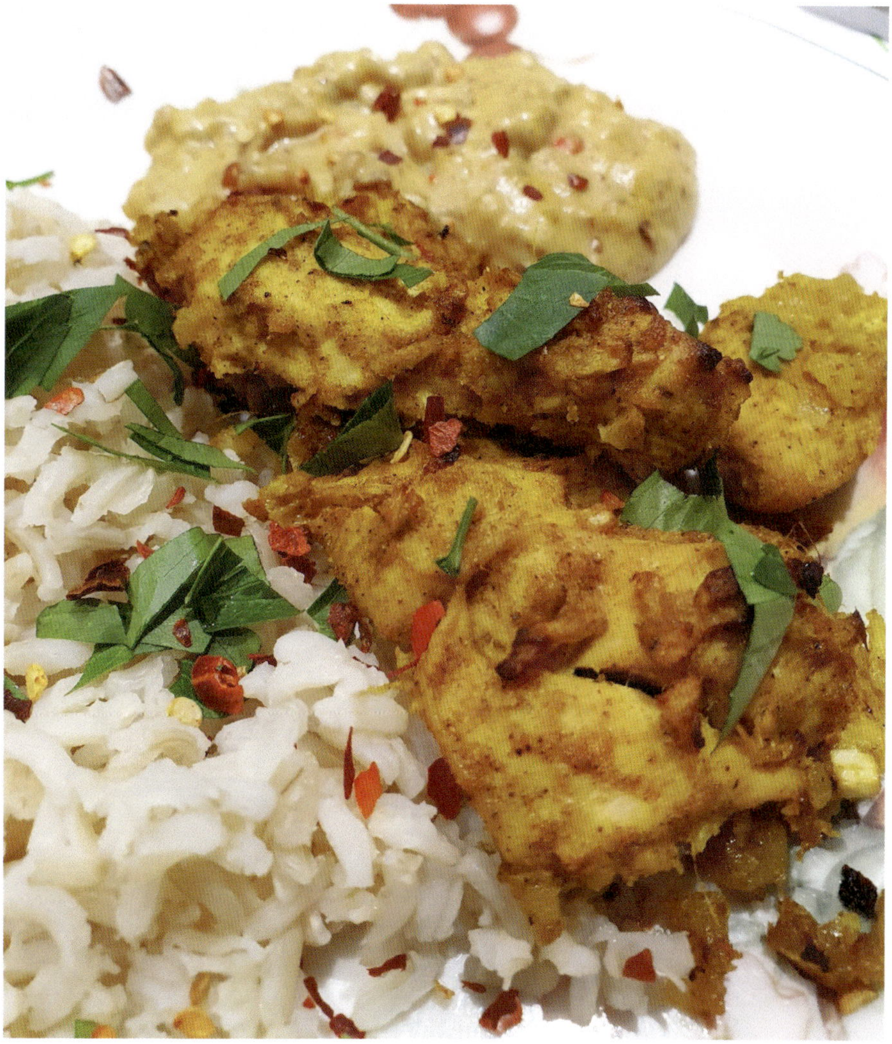

# Malaysian Satay Un-Skewered Continued

## Satay Peanut Sauce

Serves 4

*1 large onion, finely chopped*
*2 cloves of garlic creamed into a paste with a little salt*
*2 fresh chillies, finely chopped*
*1 cup coconut milk*
*1½ cups stock*
*1 tsp tamarind paste (optional) replace with a tablespoon of lime juice*
*¾ cup crunchy peanut butter*
*1 tbsp olive oil*

Prepare the sauce by softening the onion and garlic in olive oil. Add the finely chopped chillies and cook for 2 minutes. Stir in the peanut butter, coconut milk, stock and tamarind paste and bring to the boil. Simmer gently for a few minutes.

## Pineapple Salad

*Cucumber, cut into batons*
*Spring onions, finely sliced*
*Pineapple, cut into strips*
*Red chilli, finely sliced, seeds removed*
*Lettuce, washed and separated into leaves*

Arrange the cucumber and pineapple, on lettuce leaves. Scatter the finely sliced onion and fresh chilli over the salad.

When the meat Is cooked serve with the peanut sauce garnished with chopped parsley and chilli flakes, Perfect rice (page 88) and salad.

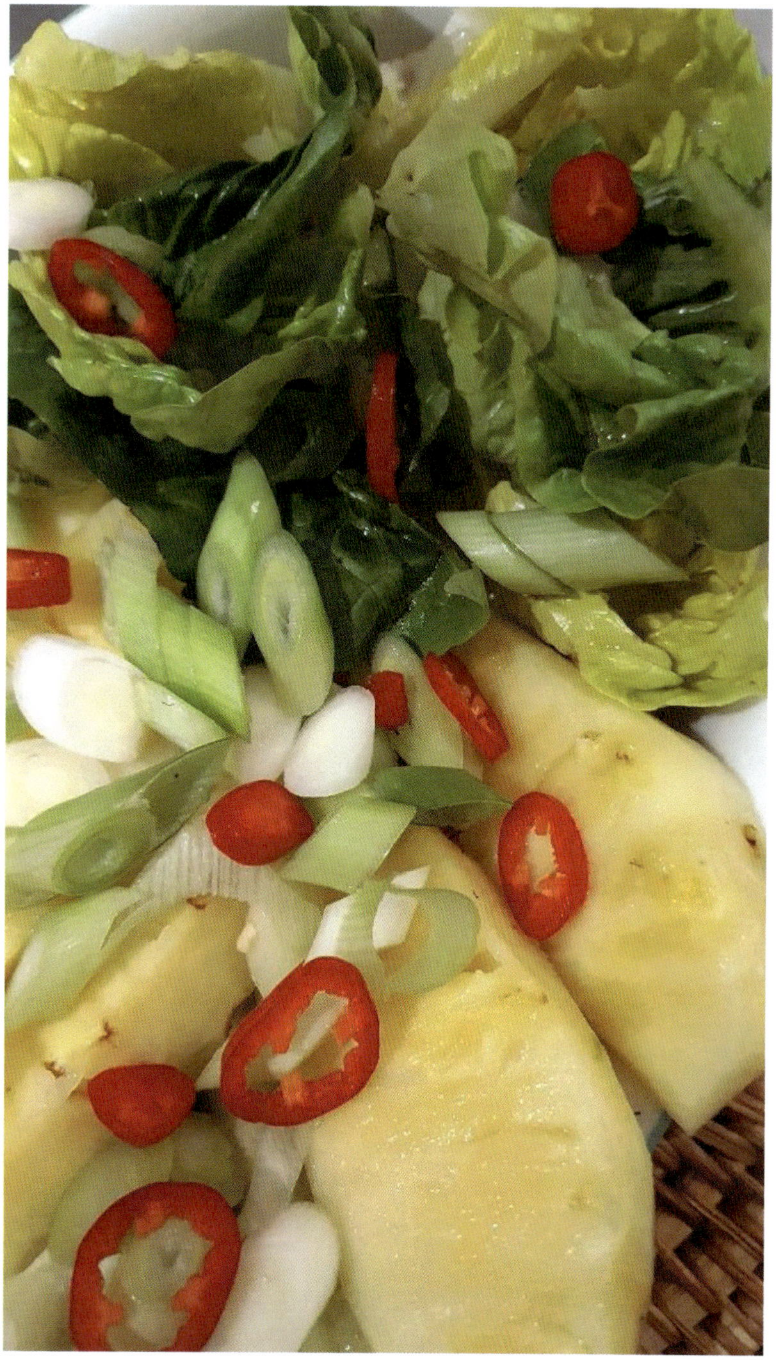

Camaret-sur-Mer, fishing boats abandoned when the sardine industry collapsed

# Laying Up Leftovers

At some stage when cruising there comes a time when we must lay-up for a period and return home so emptying out the fridge is necessary. If you are like me I dislike throwing good food away so have included a few ideas for how to use up leftovers. Imagination is the key here so something delicious is created from a mixture of leftovers which always have so much flavour. The only problem is you can't reproduce the dish twice as the leftovers will always be different.

The calm after the storm, early morning at Tighnabruaich, Bute, Scotland

# Leftovers Soup

Servings dependant on leftover food

There is no special recipe for this as it is dependant on what vegetables and meals you have leftover. Having been brought up to not waste any food this is a perfect way to make the most of your unused surplus meals. It can become more of a stew than a soup but is so satisfying with some fresh, crusty bread.

To start I mix everything together in a large saucepan. If some vegetables are too large for a soup spoon cut them up before putting in the saucepan. Top up the mixture with some stock to just cover the food and bring to the boil. To make the mixture more soup-like mash everything together. Taste it and flavour with herbs, spices, salt, pepper according to preference. Making a curry flavoured soup by adding curry paste or powder is always a favourite. Ensure that the soup has sufficient liquid so it is a soup consistency and boil well. This is a truly delicious way to use up unused cooked food.
Serve hot with crusty bread, a sandwich, croutons, a little grated cheese, a spoonful of natural yoghurt, the list is endless.

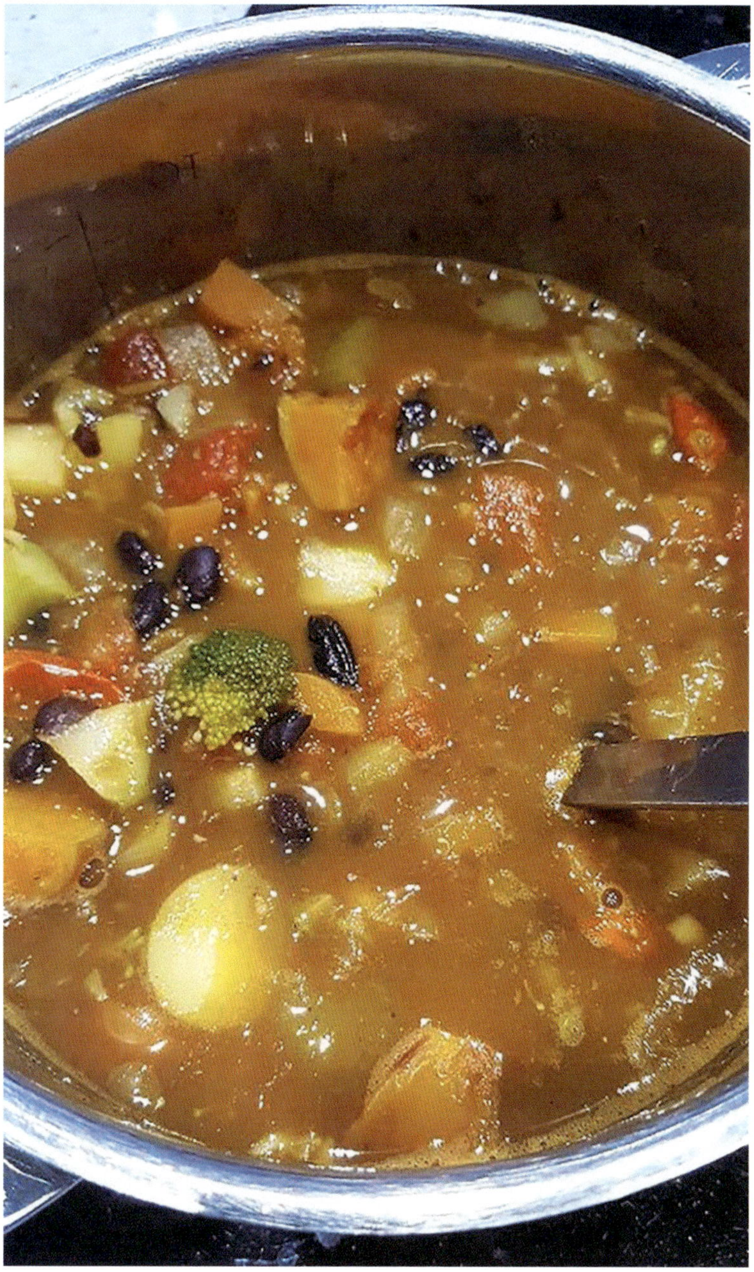

# Laying Up Cottage Pie

Servings dependant on leftover food
The 24cm dish filled will serve 4

Having sailed from Plymouth to St Helier via Portland, Alderney to Guernsey on to St Helier, Jersey there were several leftover one pot meals that were not enough on their own for a meal for the crew. So they were all combined in a deep casserole dish and topped with sliced leftover potatoes a little grated cheese and baked together 180°C, 160°C fan, Gas 4, until the potatoes were golden.

A tip here is to heat up the unused food in a saucepan so that it is hot, then put it into the casserole dish and top with the potatoes as it takes a long time to heat through in the small oven onboard and you do want it to be piping hot. When reheating food it must be heated all the way through and come to boiling point as you don't want any crew with upset stomachs.

Serve with a selection of steamed vegetables such as kale, carrots, broccoli, cabbage, peas or roast some butternut squash alongside the cottage pie. Use whatever you have on board and don't forget a jug of hot gravy. Either make your own if space and time permit or use a good instant gravy .

A word of caution here:  If you are uncertain as to whether the left overs are edible don't include them.  I have a saying "if in doubt, leave it out".  Better to be safe than ill.

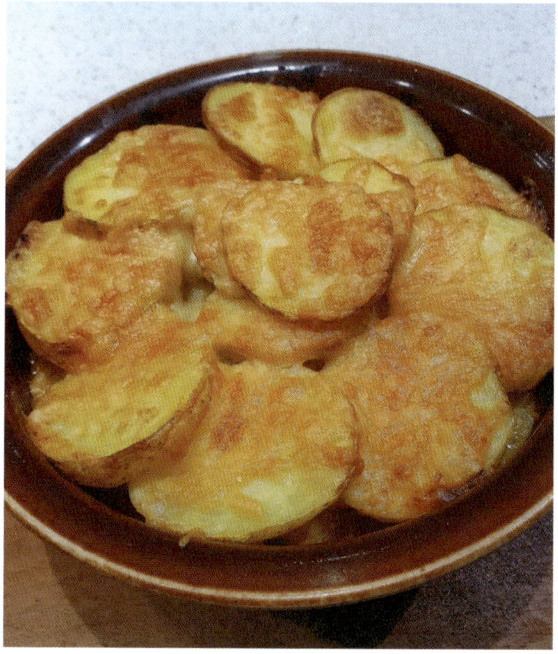

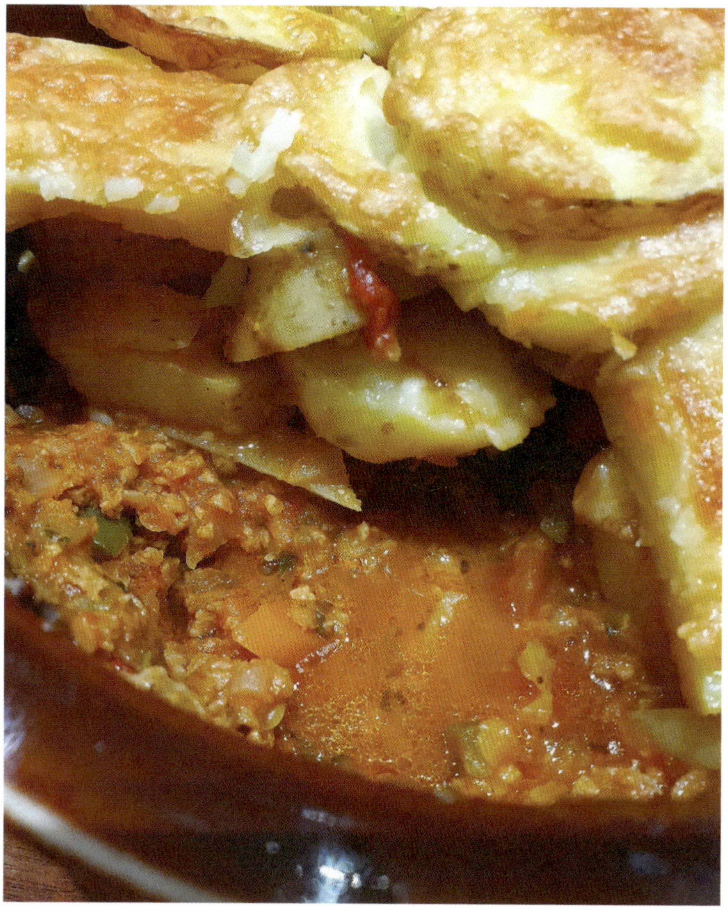

# Paella de Sobras

Servings dependant on leftover food

This is usually the final dish made with everything that is left in the fridge and is accompanied by a stir-fry of leftover fresh vegetables or salad. Throw everything in as it really is a tasty way to eat surplus food and it brings all the flavours together to make a savoury rice.

Take one or two finely sliced onions add 2 or 3 cloves of crushed garlic and soften in a large saucepan, until translucent, in a few tablespoons of olive oil. Add any raw ingredients to the onion such as a peppers, mushrooms, carrots, tomatoes and continue cooking with the lid on until the vegetables are partially cooked. Add any meat that you have left over in the fridge such as sliced ham or chicken, olives, artichoke hearts, together with ½ cup of rice per person. Cook gently for a couple of minutes and then add 1 cup of stock to every cup of rice. Bring to the boil and lower the heat. Add some herbs, pepper, salt to taste, any spices, a little chilli and simmer gently until the rice is cooked. Approximately 15 minutes for white rice and 25 minutes for wholemeal rice.

Serve with a salad or stir-fry of left over vegetables.

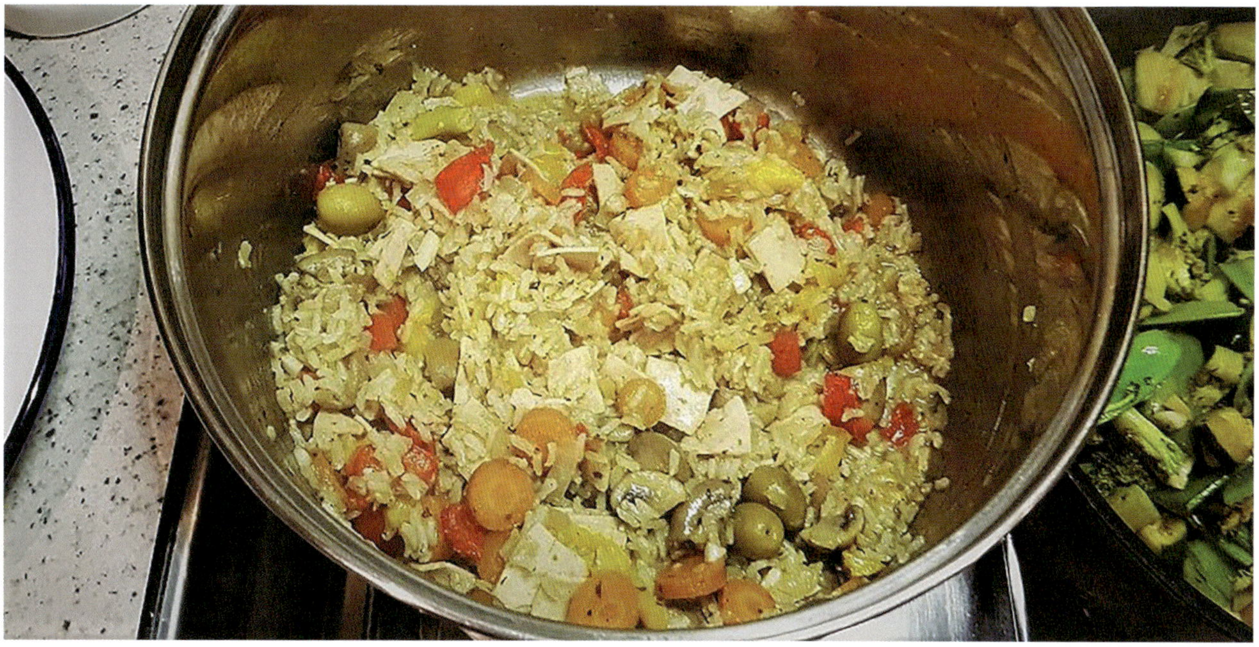

# Laying Up Quiche

### Serves 4

This is a delicious way to use up several meals or vegetables that have been left over.  Combine them in a crust and sprinkle with a little cheese.  It is delicious hot or cold and can be taken with you as lunch when travelling home.

*1 quick pastry crust baked blind  (page 160) in 24cm dish*
*Grated cheese*
*Sufficient leftover meals to fill the pastry crust*

I used left over vegetarian chilli, vegetarian mince and some cooked broccoli and butternut squash.  It is amazing how delicious a combination like this is.  When you have baked the pastry crust take out of the oven and fill with the leftover food that has been mixed together.  Cut any large pieces of vegetables so that the filling has a fairly smooth texture.  Top with grated cheese and put into a moderately hot oven 160°C, 140°C fan, Gas 3 until the cheese has melted and changed colour approximately 30 minutes.  If you find there is insufficient filling just beat 2 eggs and combine with a little milk and top the filling with this mixture. Sprinkle with cheese and bake in the usual way. Serve hot or cold with salad.

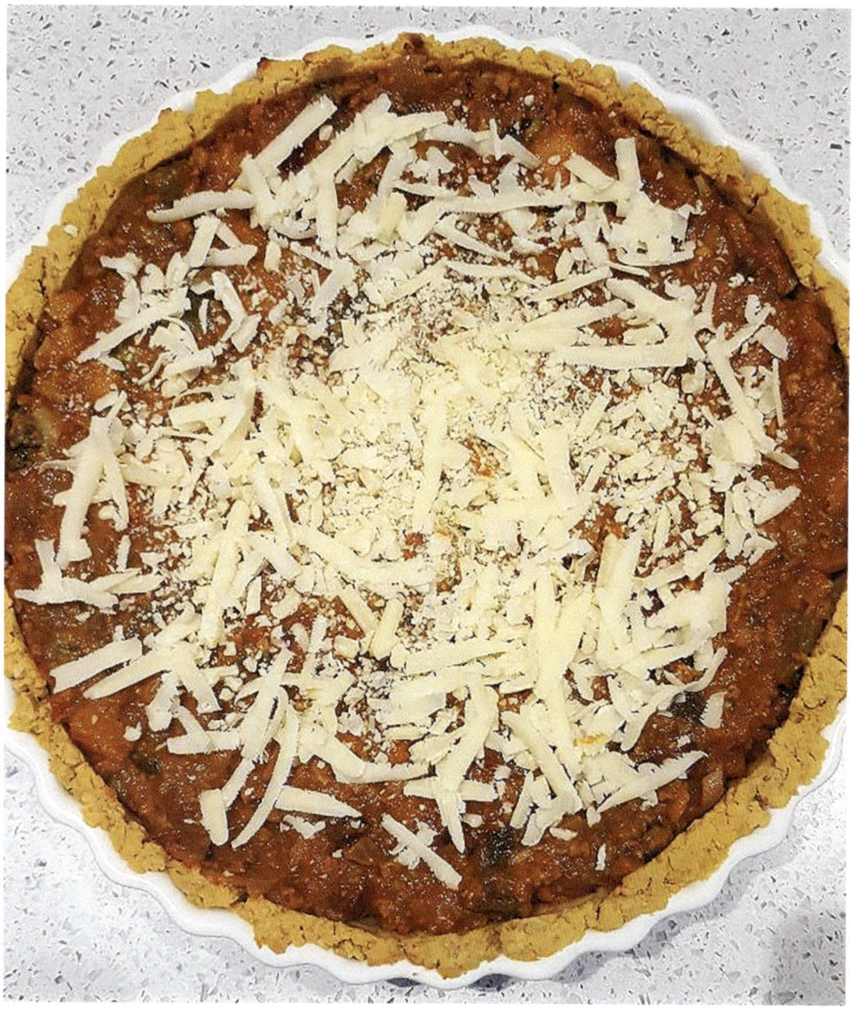

Afternoon tea at Audierne after sailing through the Raz du Seine

# Desserts

A dessert is the perfect way to round off a good meal especially if it has been a hard sail. There is nothing like a sweet treat to make it all seem worthwhile. I have found that when travelling beautiful, easy desserts are available in the local supermarket such as petit pot de crème au chocolat, crème aux oeufs, crème caramel, small apple pies or crumbles. Not to mention the exquisite fruit tartelettes, cakes and pastries that can be found in all towns in Europe. If you are unprepared here are a few suggestions.

When provisioning stock up on a few tins of fruit such as peaches , apricots, apple pie filling, mango slices, cherries and summer fruits in fruit juice. They can satisfy that desire for a dessert when used in some of the recipes that follow or just topped with yoghurt or custard.

# Fruit Fool

Serves 4

A simple but delicious dessert made with equal parts custard and fruit puree. To add texture and make it special serve with a biscuit such as a cigarette russe, tuiles or langue de chat. The fruit puree can be made from stewed apples, gooseberries, prunes, apricots, cherries or mashed banana as well as sieved strawberries, raspberries, blueberries, kiwi fruit. The quantities below are a guide and should be ample for 4 servings and the secret is to have equal portions of custard and puree.

To 500g of custard add 500g of fruit puree in a large bowl. Keep a small amount of the puree to one side. Stir the puree into the custard until combined and spoon into 4 serving dishes. Put a teaspoonful of the reserved puree in the centre of the fool and create a swirl. Sprinkle with flaked almonds and serve with a biscuit.

If you wish you can put some broken biscuit at the bottom of the serving dish so that you have a little more texture or some soft fruit to give it colour.

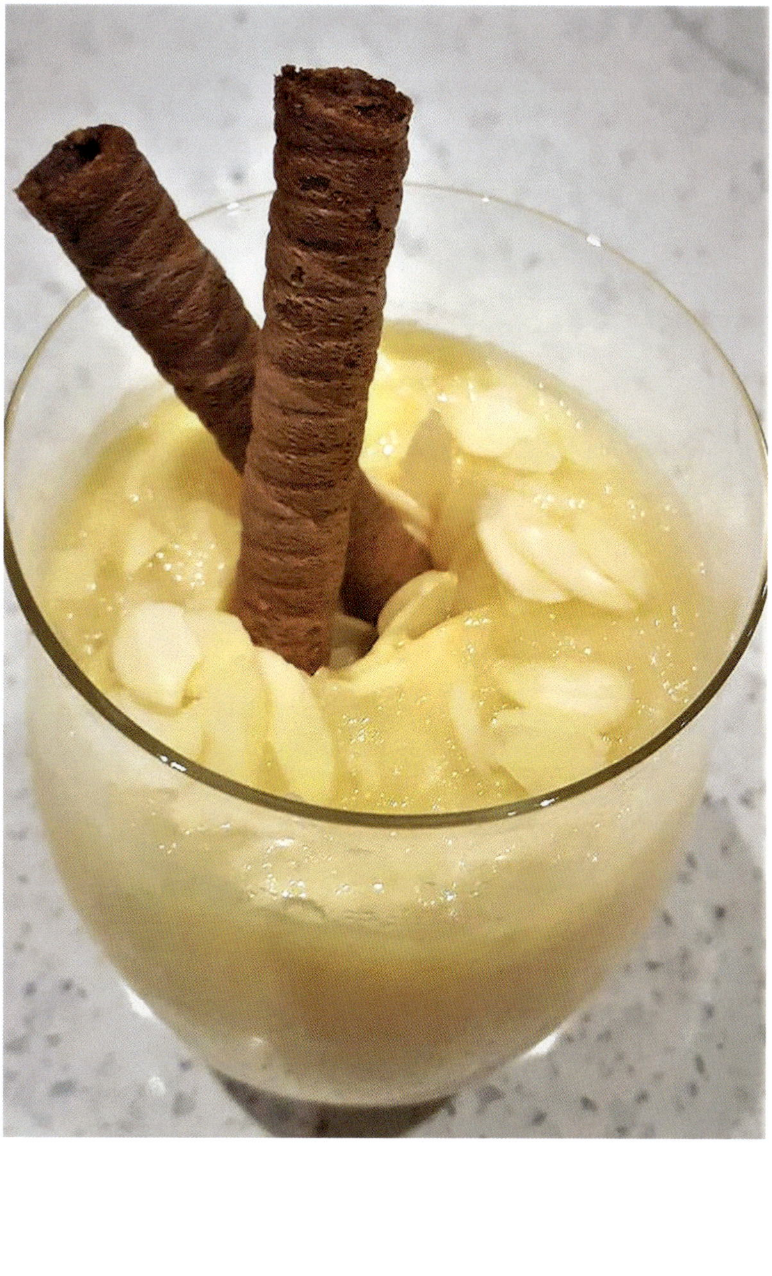

# Fruit Crumble

Serves 4

This can be prepared with any seasonal fruit. I made this with plums which were readily available and in abundance. The addition of prunes is inspired by travelling down the coast of Brittany where they are used in many of their desserts. The quantities in this recipe are a guide and dependant on how many the crumble is prepared for. Make individual crumbles if you have sufficient ovenproof dishes on board such as silicone muffin containers.

Wash 800g of plums and quarter, removing the stone. Place in a saucepan with a handful of halved prunes, add 50g brown sugar to sweeten, a cinnamon stick, a little water and put on a gentle heat. Simmer until just soft. This should take 15—20 minutes. When cooked spoon into a suitable oven proof container; I used a loaf tin. Put 300g granola into a basin and add chopped nuts, seeds such as sesame, sunflower and pumpkin, sprinkle with ground cinnamon, nutmeg and a little more brown sugar. Mix together well and spoon over the plums. Place in a medium oven 160°C, 140°C fan, Gas mark 3 for 25—30 minutes until heated through and the granola is crisp. Serve with custard, yoghurt or cream.

139

# Seafarers Trifle

*Serves 1*

A delicious dessert that can be made using ingredients you have on board. You can accommodate different likes and dislikes to make an individual sweet for each member of the crew.

Take one madeleine cake per person and slice it. Place in the bottom of an individual bowl or glass. Soak the cake with a couple of teaspoons of fruit juice, sherry or a spirit if you have them on board, and if it is not for a child. Pour a generous serving of custard over the cake to cover. Place sliced soft fruit over the custard such as strawberries, raspberries, sliced kiwi fruit, nectarines, banana or plums. Top with a crème caramel and cover this with yoghurt. Sprinkle with chopped nuts and seeds and place a square of chocolate in the centre.

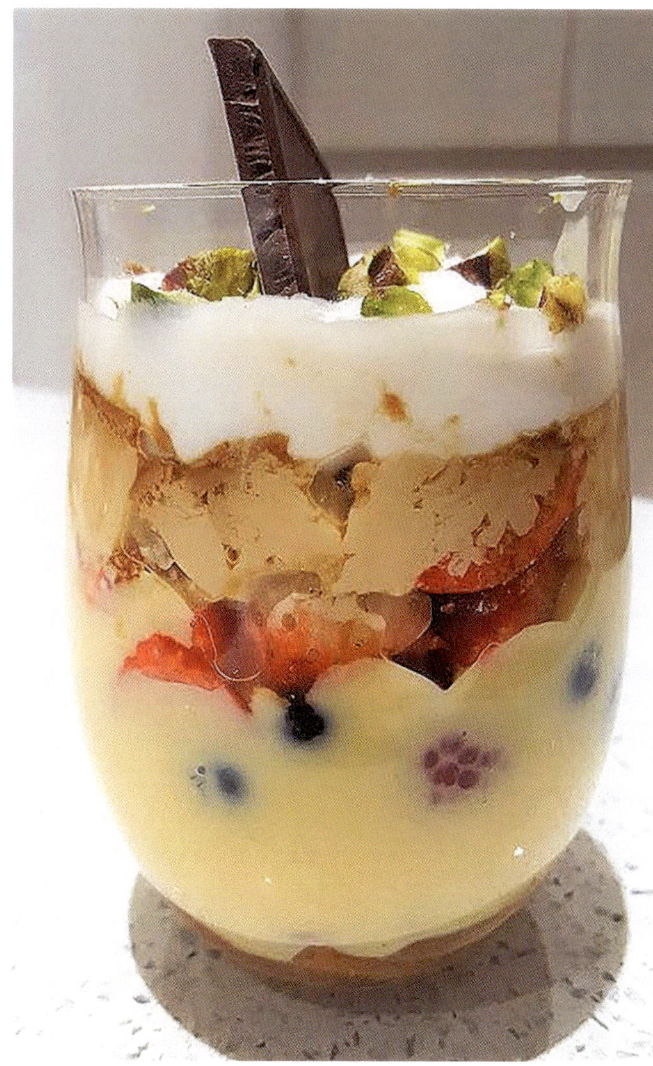

# Apricot Almond Baked Custard

## Serves 4

A delicious dessert which can be made if stormbound and cooking helps to while away the time. I made this dessert with whole apricots but it would be equally delicious to add chopped apricots to the mixture before pouring into a silicone cup and it would be easier to eat.

*500g ready made custard*
*8 dried apricots, chopped*
*50g ground almonds*
*2 eggs*

Preheat the oven to 160°C, 140°C fan, Gas 3. Sprinkle the chopped dried apricots in the bottom of either individual silicone ovenproof cups or in one larger ovenproof dish. (The apricots can be left whole and placed at the bottom of the dish or chopped and mixed into the custard.) To 500g ready made custard add 50g ground almonds or other ground nuts and 2 well beaten eggs. Pour this mixture evenly over the dried apricots in the silicone cups and place on an oven proof tray. Pour a little water in the oven proof tray surrounding the silicone cups to make a bain marie and bake in the moderate preheated oven 160°C, 140°C fan, Gas 3 for 30—40 minutes or until set. Makes 4 servings. Serve either warm or cold.

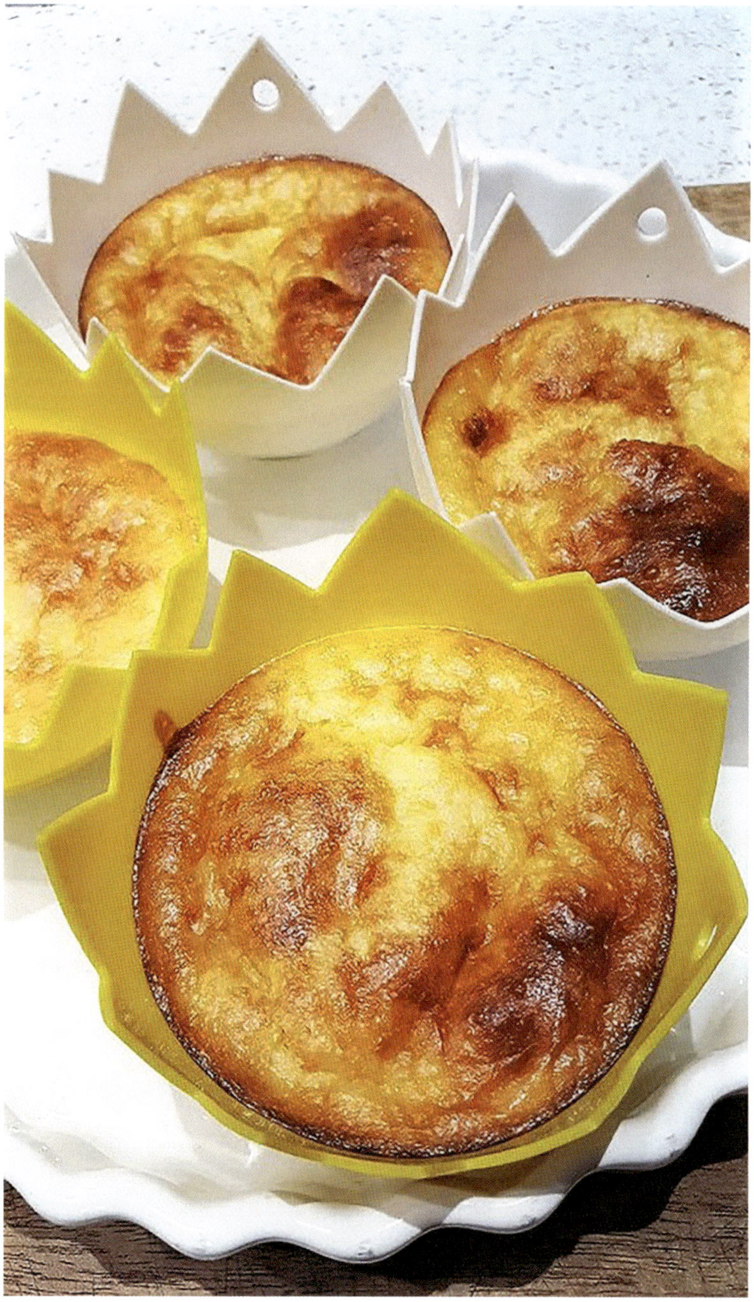

# Chocolate Indulgence

Serves 1

No dessert section would be complete without a chocolate sweet. This easy combination will please all chocolate lovers. It is very rich so make it in small dishes.

*1 chocolate brownies or small slices of chocolate cake, per person*
*Fruit juice or sherry*
*Chocolate custard*
*Raspberries or strawberries*
*Chopped nuts*
*1 small chocolate mousse per person*
*Plain yogurt*
*Dark chocolate for grating*

Slice the chocolate brownie and place in the bottom of a glass or serving dish. Pour a tablespoon of fruit juice or sherry over the brownie. Generously spoon over chocolate custard to cover the cake. Cover the custard with whole raspberries or sliced strawberries and chopped nuts. Top this with an individual chocolate mousse and spoonful of plain yoghurt and grated chocolate. Serves 1.

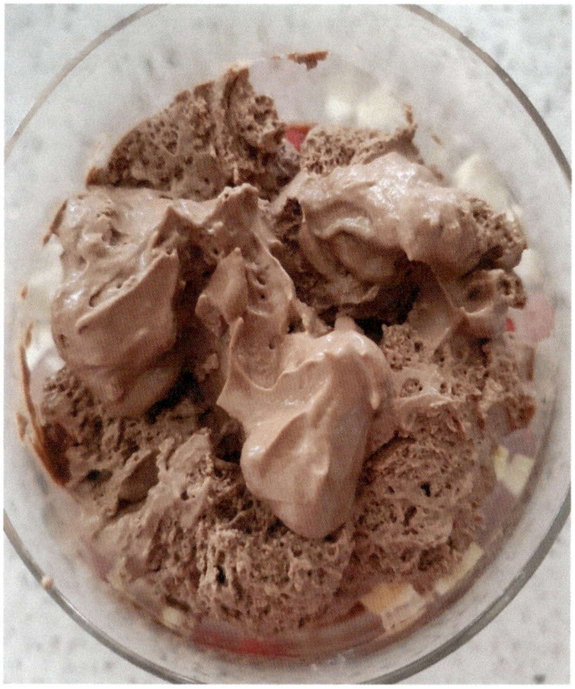

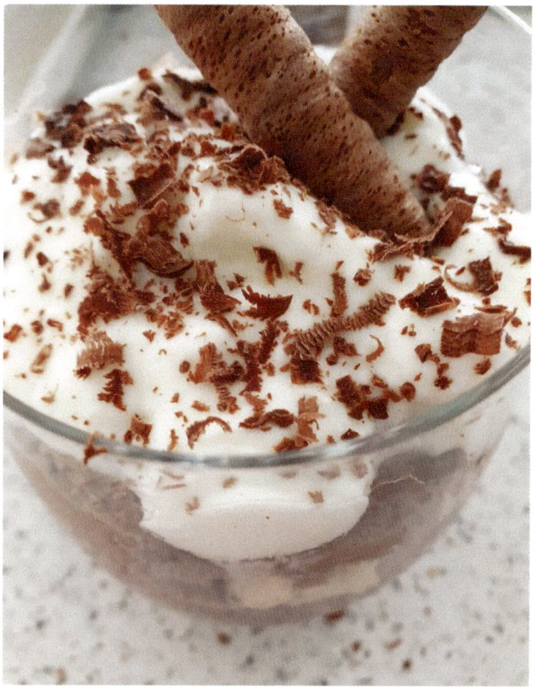

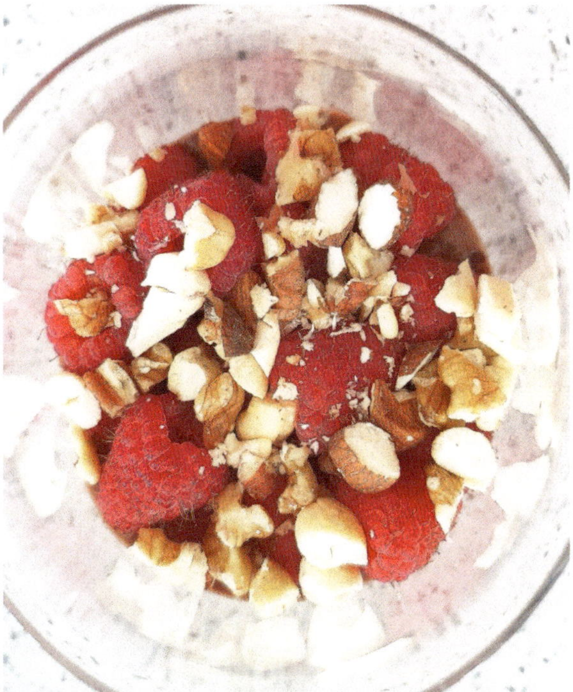

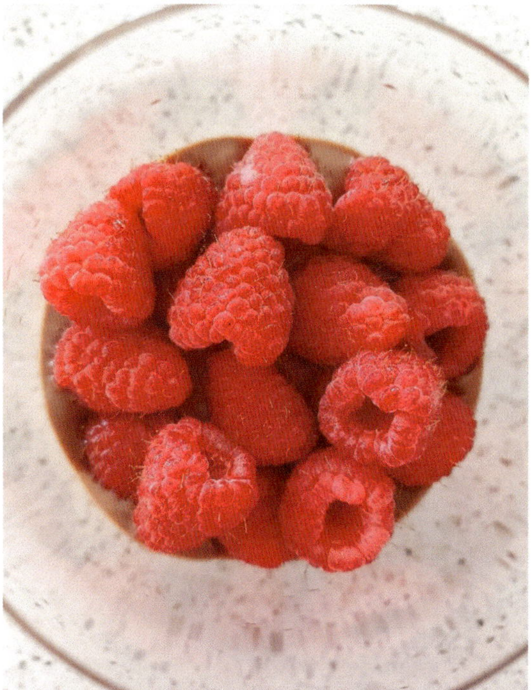

Entrance to Vieux-Port de La Rochelle

# Baking Bread and Cakes

There are occasions when it is not possible to sail because of bad weather and spending some of this time baking alleviates boredom apart from being very satisfying. Whether tied to a mooring, at anchor or attached to a pontoon making a loaf of bread or some muffins gives a lovely homely smell of baking and provides freshly made bakes. I have chosen recipes that don't require a food mixer and are easily mixed such as batters or rubbing in to make a cake mixture .

Having lived on board for several weeks we missed a fresh loaf of bread. It is one of the pleasures of cooking on board to produce a loaf of bread in cramped conditions. The dough cannot be made with a food mixer unless your galley is well equipped and you have shore power. Half a 1.5kg bag will make a good sized loaf and will rise beautifully using one sachet of dried yeast.

The temperatures given are for recipes using an electric oven as well as gas in case you bake at home. You may wish to invest in an oven thermometer to get to know how to regulate your onboard gas oven.

# Wheaty Fruit Loaf

Serves 6—8

This loaf is a perfect way to use up stale wheat biscuit cereal and makes a great breakfast on the go topped with mashed or sliced banana. It is satisfying and nutritious as well as requiring minimum preparation   The dried fruit can be varied depending on what is available on board and the ease of preparation means it can be baking while you are underway or safely anchored.

*4 wheat biscuits cereal, (Weetabix)*
*1 cup of dark brown sugar*
*½ cup of chopped apricots*
*½ cup raisins*
*1 ½ cups of milk, dairy or almond, coconut etc.*
*2 tablespoons sunflower seeds, chopped nuts or mixed seeds*
*1 cup of wholemeal self raising flour*
*1 teaspoon baking powder*
*2 teaspoons ground cinnamon*

Mix the crumbled wheat biscuits, apricots, raisins, cinnamon, sunflower seeds and sugar in a bowl.  Add the milk and leave until it has been completely absorbed.  You can leave this to soak overnight or to speed up the process the milk can be warmed and then the mixture allowed to cool.  It should be thick and the milk absorbed by the other ingredients.  Grease a loaf tin  and heat the oven to moderate 180°C, 160°C fan, Gas mark 4.  Fold in the flour and baking powder until just combined into the wet ingredients and put into the prepared loaf tin. Bake for 50—60 minutes or until a skewer comes out clean.  Leave to cool.  Delicious with butter.

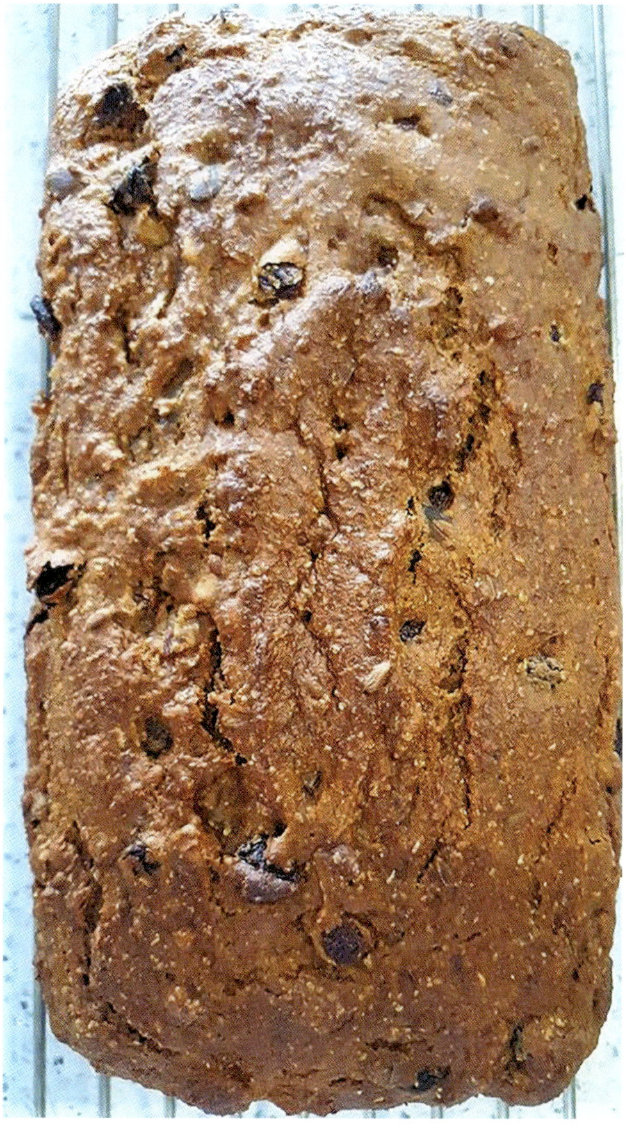

# Beetroot and Chocolate Muffins

Makes 12

Just before our journey to the Scilly Isles I harvested my large crop of beetroot grown in the garden and took some of them with us. When stormbound in Padstow I used some of the beetroot to make these muffins. They are quick to make and the chocolate perfectly compliments the earthy beetroot making them moist and indulgent. Delicious with a hot drink or as a dessert with raspberries and cream or Greek yoghurt.

*3 eggs*
*200g molasses sugar*
*200 ml olive oil*
*200g wholemeal self raising flour*
*130g grated plain chocolate or chocolate chips*
*130g grated beetroot*
*1 teaspoon baking powder*
*1 teaspoon vanilla*
*12 dark cocoa discs*

Prepare all the ingredients before starting the cake by grating the beetroot and chocolate. Put paper cases into the muffin/cupcake tin. Light the oven to a medium heat, 180°C, 160°C fan, Gas mark 4. Mix the flour, baking powder, sugar, and chocolate in a mixing bowl. Add the grated beetroot and mix well. Whisk the eggs with a fork or hand whisk and add the oil whisking until combined. Pour the mixture into the dry ingredients and fold in until just combined. Spoon mixture into the paper cases leaving them ¾ full. Place the tin on the middle shelf of the oven and bake for 15 to 20 minutes or until firm to the touch. Immediately after removing muffins from oven place a cocoa disc in the middle of each cake and leave to cool.

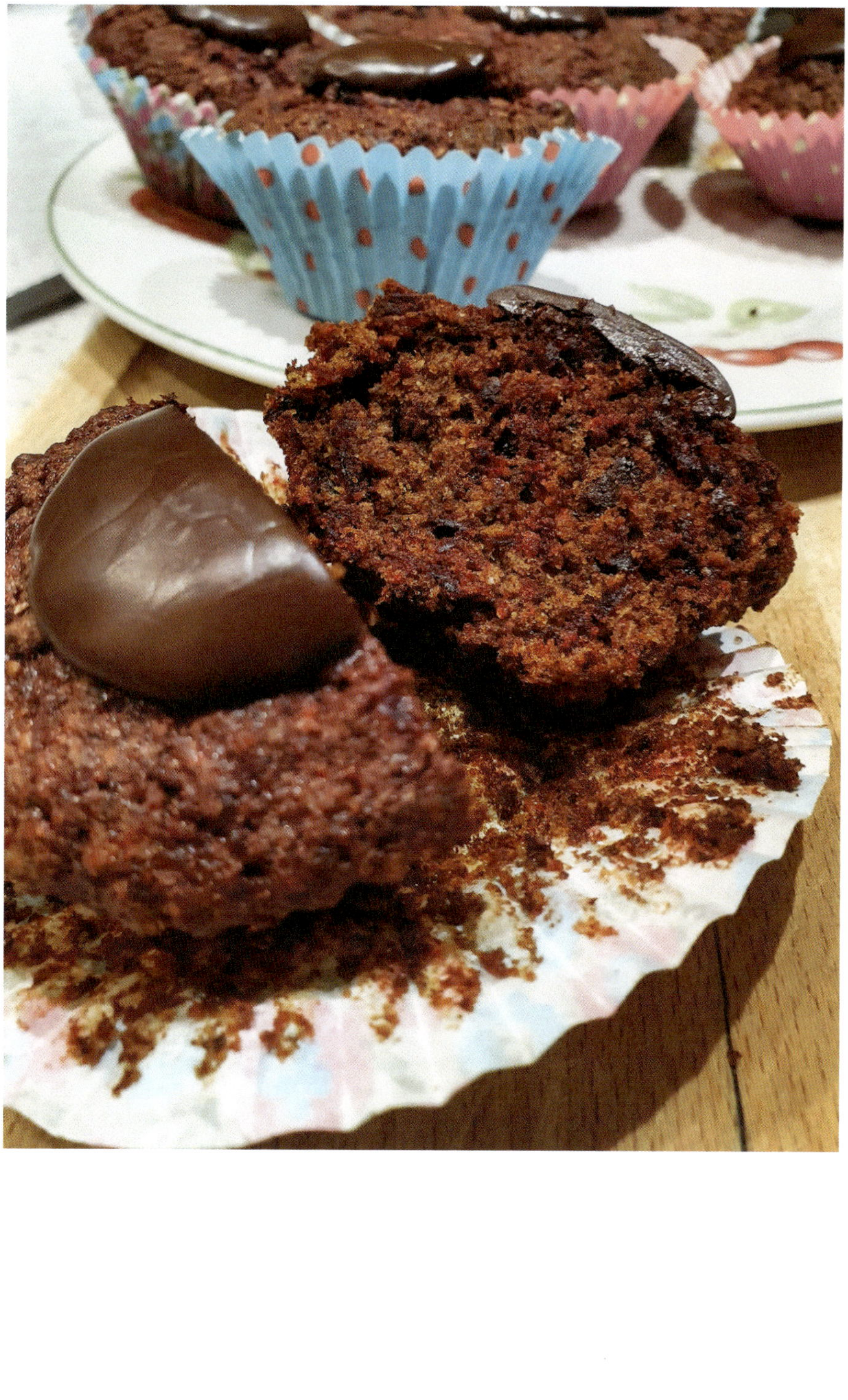

# Breton Fruit Cake

Serves 8—10

Inspired by Far Breton, a traditional cake from Brittany, while sailing down the north west coast of France where prunes are a favourite in Breton cookery. An easy cake to make and perfect for storing for a few days in an air tight container. Delicious with a slice of cheddar cheese and an apple for a quick snack when underway and there is little time for food preparation. Use any dried fruit such as, sultanas, raisins, currents, dried apricots or dried mango cut into small pieces, whatever you have on board.

*170g butter*
*170g molasses sugar*
*340g wholemeal self raising flour*
*3 eggs*
*240g dried fruit*
*100g prunes cut in half*
*90g nuts, roughly chopped*
*142 ml milk*

Heat the oven to 180°C, 160°C fan, Gas 4, and grease a 17 cm cake tin. Put the flour into a bowl and add the butter. Rub the butter into the flour until it resembles fine breadcrumbs. Mix in the sugar, dried fruit, nuts and stir well. Beat the eggs well and add the milk. Stir into the cake mixture until just combined. Spoon into the cake tin and bake for approximately 1¼ hours until cooked. A skewer inserted into the middle of the cake should come out clean.

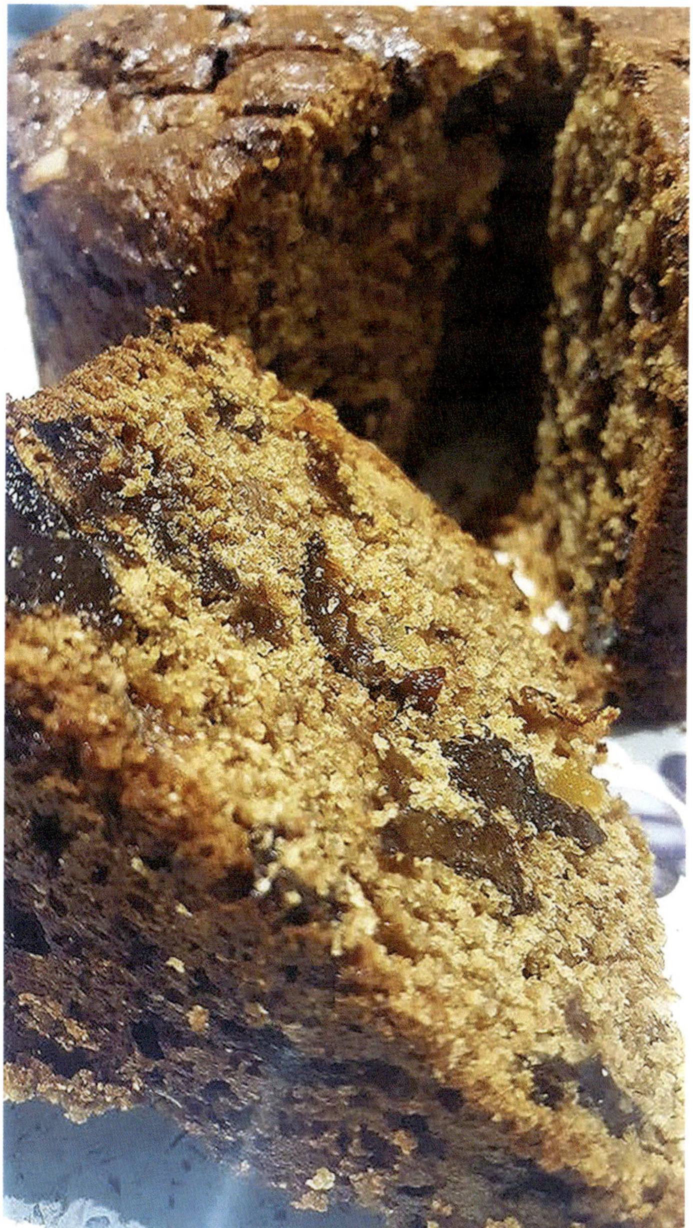

# Devon Apple Blueberry Cake

Serves 8—10

This makes a delicious dessert or teatime treat. Use any apples you have to hand. Serve it with custard, yoghurt, cream or ice cream.

*225g wholemeal self raising flour*
*1 tsp ground cinnamon*
*1 tsp mixed spice*
*100g molasses sugar*
*100g butter*
*250g apples*
*100g blueberries*
*Flaked almonds*
*1 egg*

Grease a loaf tin or 17 cm cake tin  Heat the oven to 190°C, 170°C fan, Gas 5. Mix the dry ingredients together and add the butter. Rub the butter into dry ingredients until they resemble fine breadcrumbs. Wash and chop the apple and add to the dry ingredients with the blueberries, and beaten egg. Fold together, the mixture should be moist and stick together. If a little dry add 2 tablespoon of milk. When baking, the juice from the apple and blueberries provides some moisture so don't add too much liquid. Spoon into a prepared tin and spread evenly. Sprinkle with flaked almonds and place in a preheated oven for approximately 40—50 minutes until risen, firm to the touch and a skewer inserted in the middle comes out clean. Cool in the tin before turning out.

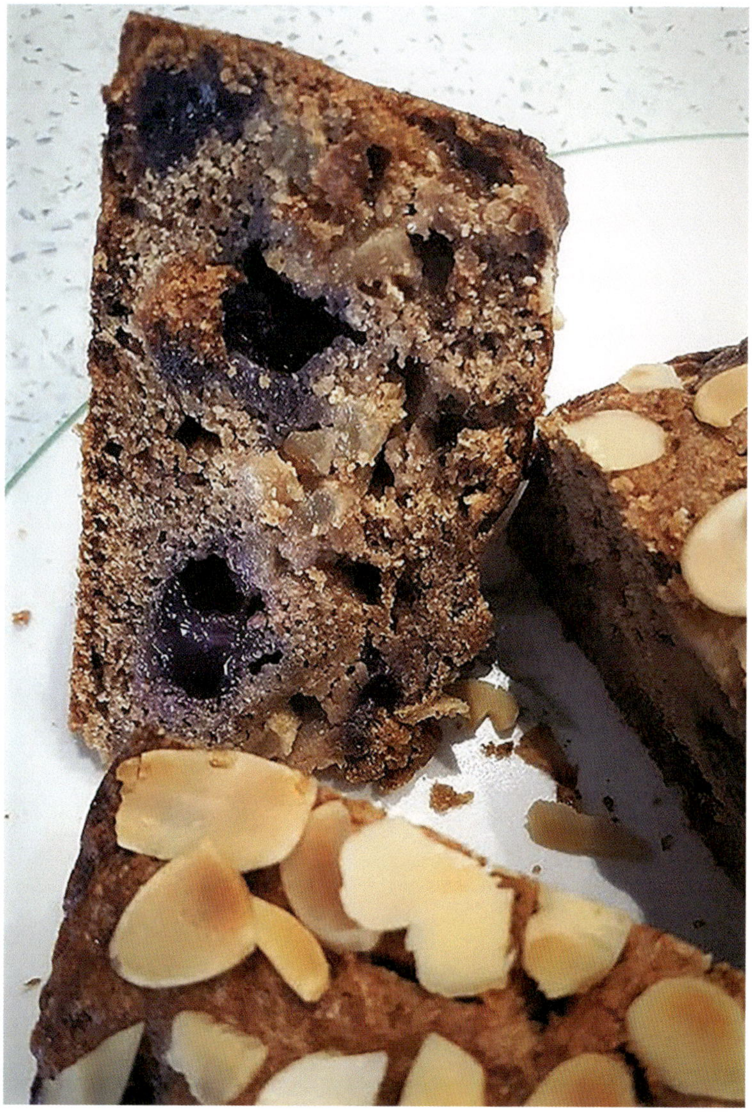

# Bananajack

## Makes 9 -12 squares approximately

Always a favourite as a sweet snack.  The bananas give the flapjack moisture so less  butter or coconut oil are needed.  The seeds give a nutty texture and added nutrition.

*3 ripe bananas*
*85g molasses sugar*
*85g golden syrup*
*227g rolled oats*
*2 tbsp coconut oil or butter*
*60g mixed seeds*

Heat oven to 190°C, 170°C fan, Gas 5.  Put the sugar, molasses and coconut oil in a saucepan.  Heat very gently stirring until the sugar is dissolved.  Do not let it boil.  Remove from the heat and add the oats and mashed banana.  Stir well and spoon into a square 24 cm dish and bake for 25-30 minutes until golden.  Mark into squares while still warm.  Makes 9—12 squares.  Store in an airtight container.

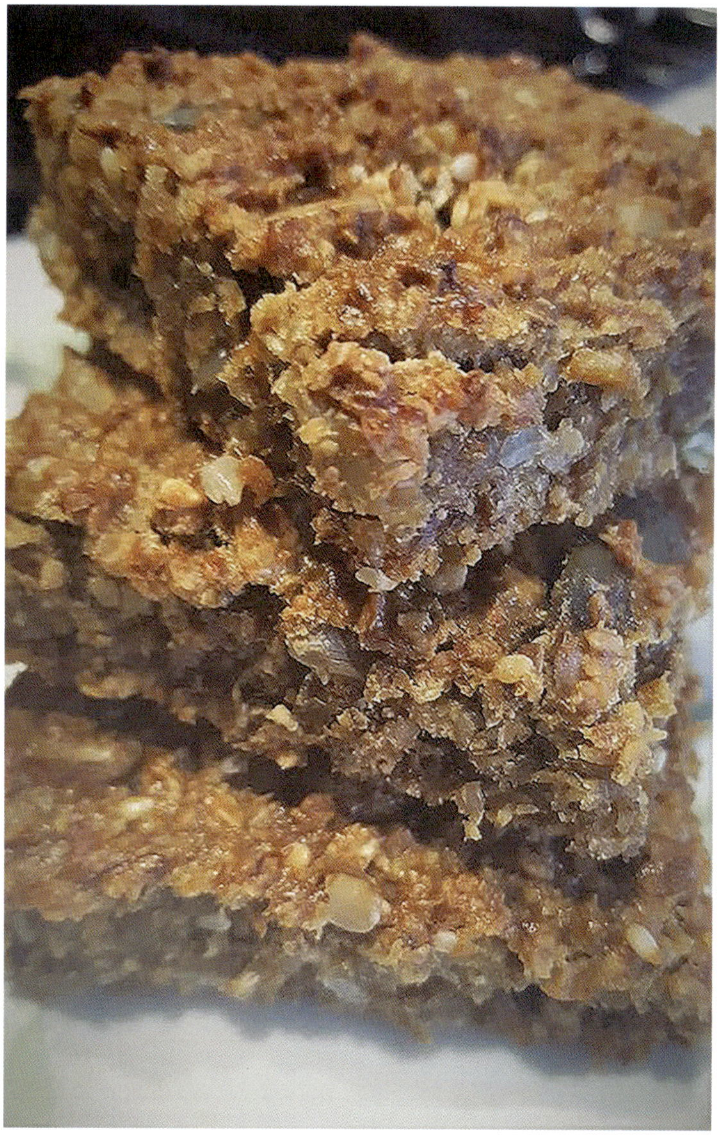

# Cheesy Oat Squares

9 –12 squares

A nutritious snack for those who prefer something savoury and a great accompaniment to soup or salads.  Store in an air tight container in the cool box and it will keep for several days.

*300g rolled oats*

*200g grated carrots*

*200g grated cheese*

*50g mixed seeds*

*50g sundried tomatoes in oil, chopped*

*50g nuts (any type of nuts)*

*4 tsp dried rosemary*

*100g butter, melted*

Heat the oven to 180°C, 160°C fan, Gas 4.  Melt the butter in a saucepan big enough to take all the ingredients. Add the rest of the ingredients and stir well.  If the mixture is a little dry add a little of the sundried tomato oil until the mixture sticks together. Spoon into a prepared 24 cm square dish and press well.  Bake for about 40 minutes until it has changed colour to a golden brown.  Cut into squares while warm.

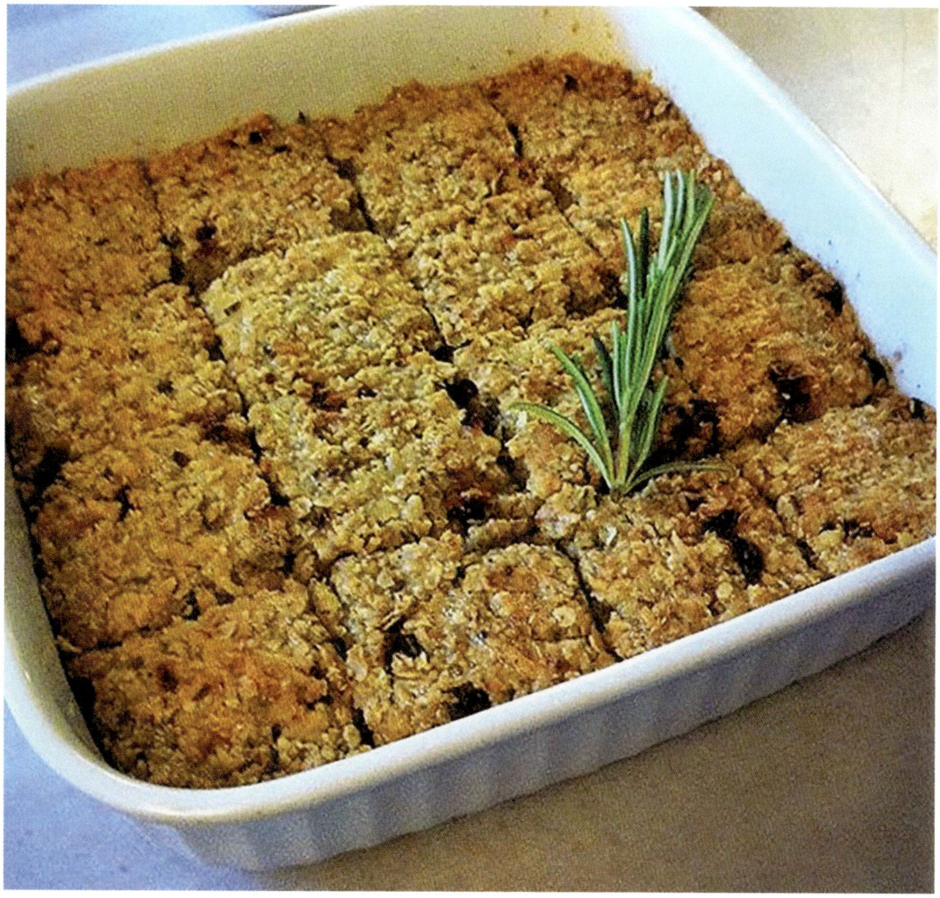

# Quick Pastry Crust

A quick pastry crust for making on board which doesn't need rolling out and can be used for sweet tarts or savoury quiches. Press into the dish with a spoon for a quick delicious and nourishing crust.

*150g red lentils*
*1¾ cups water*
*50g oats*
*50g ground almonds*
*Seasoning*

Put lentils in a saucepan with the water and bring to the boil. Boil for 5 minutes and then reduce the heat and cook for a further 10 minutes or until the lentils look like a porridge. Take off the heat and add the oats mixing in well. Then stir in the ground almonds. Mix until all the ingredients are combined and dough-like. Use as required. Season to taste.

For a quiche or tart press into a flan dish with a fork and bake blind at 190°C, 170°C fan, gas mark 5, for 15 minutes before filling. Lines a 24 cm dish.

Apple, Cranberry and Almond Fruit Tart made with quick pastry crust

# Wholemeal Bread

Approximately 12 slices

*750g strong stoneground wholemeal flour*
*7g dried yeast*
*2 tbsp olive oil*
*2 tsps brown sugar*
*1 tsp salt*
*450ml warm water*

Add the dried yeast to the wholemeal flour and mix well with a wooden spoon.  Add 2 tablespoons of olive oil and mix in.  In a measuring jug, add the sugar and salt to the warm water and mix well until the sugar and salt are dissolved.  Make a well in the centre of the flour and pour in 335ml of the water.  Make a paste by stirring and mixing the flour gradually into the water to form dough.  Add more water until the dough is soft but firm.  Knead the dough for 10 minutes until it is smooth. Leave the dough in the bowl covered with a damp tea towel to double in size.  About 40 minutes.  Turn out onto a floured surface and knead gently.  Shape the dough and put into an oiled bread tin.  (Alternately cut in half and form 2 round flat loaves.  Place on a greased baking sheet.)  Cover with the damp tea towel and leave in a warm place until doubled in size.  Uncover and brush with a little cold water and sprinkle sesame seeds on top.

Bake in a hot preheated oven 220°C, 200°C fan, Gas mark 7, for 30-40 minutes or until cooked.  The bread should sound hollow when you tap the bottom of the loaf.

# Stages in Wholemeal Breadmaking

**Dough ready to be kneaded**

**Dough consistency**

**Dough shaped and ready for loaf tin**

**Shaped dough in tins ready for final prove**

Bread dough well risen ready for the oven

Baked and cooling wholemeal loaves

First slice cut

Round loaf baked without a bread tin

Spinach and Pesto Quiche

Apple, Cranberry and Almond Fruit Tart

Leek and Mushroom Pie made with Quick Pastry Crust (p160)

Broccoli, Tomato and Feta quiche

Entrance to Peel Harbour and Peel Castle originally constructed by Vikings, Isle of Man

Sunset at Drake Island, Plymouth Sound, at the start of our journey to La Rochelle

# Index

**A**
Almonds, flaked 136
  Fruit fool 136
  Devon apple blueberry cake 154
Almonds, ground 12
  Apricot almond baked custard 142
  Quick pastry crust 160
Almond milk 22
Allspice, ground
  Armenian lamb 116
Apple 32
  Fresh fruit salad 32
  Devon apple blueberry cake 154
Apricots, dried 12
  Middle Eastern tagine 86
  Apricot almond baked custard 142
  Wheaty fruit loaf 148
Aubergine 74
  Roasted Mediterranean vegetables 74
  Moroccan lamb with chilli, ginger 84
  Middle Eastern tagine 86
  Vegetable chilli 108
  Armenian lamb 116
Avocado 26
  Poached eggs on toast 26
  Hummus pitta with bean tabbouleh 58
  Tuna salad 64
  Mixed salad 66
  Quinoa salad 68

**B**
Baby spinach 66
  Mixed salad 66
Baked beans 12
  Gammon steak with fried egg 24
Baking powder 148
  Wheaty fruit loaf 148
  Beetroot and chocolate muffins 150
Banana 32
  Fresh fruit salad 32
  Sunflower banana toast 34
  Flapjack 156
Basil, fresh
  Fish fillets with puy lentils 102
  Laksa 112
Basmati rice 12
  Chilli con carne 88
  Balti curry 90

Pistachio pilaf 118
Bay leaves 13
  Spanish lentils with couscous
Beans in water, tinned 12
Beetroot 150
  Beetroot and chocolate muffins 150
Biscuits 12
Blueberries 32
  Fresh fruit salad 32
  Devon apple blueberry cake 154
Bouillon 12
  Chicken with noodles 110
Bread 13
Broccoli 13
  Green vegetable stir fry 72
Brownie, chocolate 144
  Chocolate indulgence 144
Bulgar wheat 58
Burgers, vegetarian 13
Butter 13
  Armenian lamb 116
  Breton fruit cake 152
  Devon apple blueberry cake 154
  Flapjack 156
  Cheesy oat squares 158
Butternut squash 13
  Quinoa salad 68
  Vegetable chilli 108

**C**
Cake 12
  Sailor's trifle 140
Cannellini beans 58
  Hummus pitta with bean tabbouleh 58
  Quinoa salad 68
Carrots 80
  Spanish lentils with couscous 80
  Penne Bolognaise 82
  Chilli con carne 88
  Balti curry 90
  Turkey braised in red wine 98
  Chicken rice 100
  Vegetarian mince 106
  Stuffed peppers 114
  Cheesy oat squares 158
Celery 106
  Vegetarian mince 106
  Chicken with noodles 110

Cereals 12
Cheese, cheddar 13
  Spinach and pesto quiche 56
  Penne Bolognaise 82
  Linguine carbonara 104
  Laying up pie 132
  Cheesy oat squares 158
Chia seeds 36
  Dawn start oats 36
Chicken 78
  Spanish chicken with peppers 78
  Chicken rice 100
  Malaysian satay 120
Chicken, cooked 110
  Chicken with noodles 110
  Laksa 112
Chickpeas 86
  Moroccan lamb with chilli, ginger 84
  Middle Eastern tagine 86
Chilli powder 108
  Vegetable chilli 108
Chillies 84
  Moroccan lamb with chilli, ginger 84
  Laksa 112
  Middle Eastern tagine 86
  Satay sauce 122
  Malaysian satay salad 122
Chilli sauce 72
  Green vegetable stir fry 72
Chocolate 140
  Sailor's trifle 140
Chocolate, dark 144
  Chocolate indulgence 144
  Beetroot and chocolate muffins 150
Chocolate mousse 144
  Chocolate indulgence 144
Chorizo 80
  Spanish lentils with couscous 80
  Chicken rice 100
Cigarette russe 136
  Fruit fool
Cinnamon, ground 13
  Spiced porridge 22
  Fruit crumble 138
  Wheaty fruit loaf 148
  Middle Eastern tagine 86
  Devon apple blueberry cake 154

Cinnamon stick 28
  Spiced dried fruit salad 28
  Fruit crumble 138
Coconut milk 122
  Satay sauce 122
Coconut oil 156
  Flapjack 156
Coffee 12
Coleslaw, red 66
Coriander, ground 120
  Malaysian satay 120
Cornflour 72
  Green vegetable stir fry 72
Courgette 72
  Green vegetable stir fry 72
  Roasted Mediterranean vegetables 74
  Spanish chicken with peppers 78
  Vegetable chilli 108
Couscous 12
  Spanish lentils with couscous 80
  Moroccan lamb with chilli, ginger 84
Cordial 12
Crème caramel 140
  Sailor's trifle 140
Cucumber 58
  Hummus pitta bean tabbouleh 58
  Tuna salad 64
  Mixed salad 66
  Malaysian satay salad 122
Cumin, ground 13
  Spiced porridge 22
  Moroccan lamb with chilli, ginger 84
  Middle Eastern tagine 86
  Chilli con carne 88
  Vegetarian mince 106
  Vegetable chilli 108
  Armenian lamb 116
  Malaysian satay 120
Currants 118
  Pistachio pilaf 118
Curry Powder 13
Custard, chocolate 144
  Chocolate indulgence 144
Custard, ready made 12
  Fruit fool 136
  Sailor's trifle 140
  Apricot almond baked custard 142

**D**
Desserts 135
Dijon mustard 66
Mixed salad 66
Dried fruit 152
  Breton fruit cake 152
Dried fruit salad 12
  Spiced dried fruit salad 28

**E**
Eggs 13
  Gammon steak with fried egg 24
  Poached eggs on toast 26
  Scrambled eggs with garlic and
    smoked salmon 42
  Spanish omelette 46
  Spinach and pesto quiche 56
  Huevos rancheros 60
  Tuna salad 64
  Linguine carbonara 104
  Apricot almond baked custard 142
  Beetroot and chocolate muffins 150
  Breton fruit cake 152
  Devon apple blueberry cake 154

**F**
Feta 56
  Spinach and pesto quiche 56
  Quinoa salad 68
Fennel 70
  Fennel and orange salad 70
Flour, white plain 94
  Hake in green sauce 94
Flour, wholemeal Self raising 148
  Wheaty fruit loaf 148
  Beetroot and chocolate muffins 150
  Breton fruit cake 152
  Devon apple blueberry cake 154
Fruit crumble 138
Fruit, fresh 13
  Fresh fruit salad 32
  Sailor's trifle 140
Fruit, puree 136
  Fruit fool 136
  Dawn start oats 36
Fruit, tinned 12

**G**
Gammon steaks with fried egg 24
Garlic 13
  Scrambled eggs garlic smoked sal 42
  Spanish omelette 46
  Spinach and pesto quiche 56
  Green vegetable stir fry 72
  Roasted Mediterranean vegetables 74
  Spanish chicken with peppers 78
Spanish lentils with couscous 80
Penne Bolognaise 82
Middle Eastern tagine 86
Chilli con carne 88
Hake in green sauce 94
Fish fillets with puy lentils 102
Vegetarian mince 106
Vegetable mince 108
Chicken with noodles 110
Stuffed peppers 114
Armenian lamb 116
Malaysian satay 120
Satay sauce 122
Ginger, fresh 13
  Spiced dried fruit salad 28
  Fresh fruit salad 32
  Moroccan lamb with chilli, ginger 84
  Middle Eastern tagine 86
  Chicken rice 100
  Fish fillets with puy lentils 102
  Chicken with noodles 110
  Laksa 112
  Malaysian satay 120
Ginger, ground 13
Golden syrup 156
  Flapjack 156
Granola 138
  Fruit crumble 138
Grapes 32
  Fresh fruit salad 32
Guacamole 88

**H**
Hake 94
  Hake in green sauce 94
Ham 100
  Chicken rice
  Linguine carbonara 104
Halloumi 13
Herbs, mixed dried 13
  Spanish lentils with couscous 80
  Chilli con carne 88
  Chicken rice 100
  Vegetarian mince 106
  Stuffed peppers 114
Hazelnuts, chopped 12
Hummus 26
  Poached eggs on toast
  Mushroom and kale eggs 30
  Hummus pitta bean tabbouleh 58

**I**

**J**

**K**

Kidney beans 88
  Chilli con carne 88
  Vegetable chilli 108
Kidney beans in chilli sauce 88
  Chilli con carne 88
Kiwi fruit 32
  Fresh fruit salad

**L**

Laying up 125
  Laying up cottage pie 128
  Laying up pie 132
Lamb 84
  Moroccan lamb with chilli, ginger 84
  Armenian lamb 116
Leftovers 125
  Leftover soup 126
  Leftovers Paella 130
Lemon 28
  Spiced dried fruit salad 28
  Fresh fruit salad 32
  Spinach with raisins and pine nuts 44
  Hummus pitta with bean tabbouleh 58
  Tuna salad 64
  Quinoa salad 68
  Chicken rice 100
  Fish fillets with puy lentils 102
  Stuffed peppers 114
  Malaysian satay 120
Lemongrass 112
  Laksa 112
Lentils puy 12
  Spanish lentils with couscous 80
  Fish fillets with puy lentils 102
Lentils, red 106
  Vegetarian mince 106
Lentils, red 12
  Quick pastry crust 160
Lettuce 64
  Tuna salad 64
  Malaysian satay salad 122
Lime 112
  Laksa 112
  Malaysian satay 120
Linguine 104
  Linguine carbonara 104

**M**

Mangetout 72
  Green vegetable stir fry 72

Laksa 112
Mango chutney 90
Marmalade 12
Marmite 12
  Vegetarian mince 106
  Vegetable chilli 108
Meat 13
Melon 32
  Fresh fruit salad
Minced meat, beef 82
  Penne Bolognaise 82
  Chilli con carne 88
Milk
  Dawn start oats 36
  Scrambled eggs with garlic and smoked salmon 42
  Spinach and pesto quiche 56
  Wheaty fruit loaf 148
  Breton fruit cake 152
Mint 58
  Hummus pitta with bean tabbouleh 58
  Fish fillets with puy lentils 102
  Laksa 112
Mixed spice 154
  Devon blueberry cake 154
Mozzarella 13
Mushrooms 13
  Gammon steak with fried egg 24
  Mushroom and kale eggs 30
  Mixed salad 66
  Turkey braised in red wine 98
  Vegetarian mince 106
  Vegetable chilli 108
Mushrooms, chestnut 112
  Laksa 112
Mustard 64
  Tuna salad 64

**N**

Naan bread 90
  Balti curry 90
Noodles 110
  Chicken with noodles 110
Noodles, rice 112
  Laksa 112
Nutmeg, ground 138
Nuts, flaked 12
Nuts, mixed 12
  Dawn start oats 36
  Quinoa salad 68
  Fruit crumble 138
  Sailor's trifle 140

Chocolate indulgence 144
Wheaty fruit loaf 148
Breton fruit cake 152
Cheesy oat squares 158
Nuts, Pistachio 118
  Pistachio pilaf 118

**O**

Oats, porridge 12
  Spiced porridge 22
  Dawn start oats 36
  Flapjack 156
  Cheesy oat squares 158
  Quick pastry crust 160
Olives 12
  Huevos rancheros 60
  Tuna salad 64
Olive oil 12
  Scrambled eggs with garlic and smoked salmon 42
  Spinach with raisins and pine nuts 44
  Spanish omelette 46
  Spinach and pesto quiche 56
  Huevos rancheros 60
  Tuna salad 64
  Mixed salad 66
  Quinoa salad 68
  Fennel and orange salad 70
  Green vegetable stir fry 72
  Roasted Mediterranean vegetables 74
  Spanish chicken with peppers 78
  Spanish lentils with couscous 80
  Penne Bolognaise 82
  Moroccan lamb with chilli, ginger 84
  Middle Eastern tagine 86
  Chilli con carne 88
  Balti curry 90
  Hake in green sauce 94
  Turkey braised in red wine 98
  Chicken rice 100
  Fish fillets with puy lentils 102
  Linguine carbonara 104
  Vegetarian mince 106
  Vegetable chilli 108
  Laksa 112
  Stuffed peppers 114

Armenian lamb 116
Pistachio pilaf 118
Malaysian satay 120
Satay sauce 122
Beetroot and chocolate muffins 150
Wholemeal bread 162
Onions 13
  Spanish omelette 46
  Spinach and pesto quiche 56
  Hummus pitta bean tabbouleh 58
  Tuna salad 64
  Quinoa salad 68
  Green vegetable stir fry 72
  Roasted Mediterranean vegetables 74
  Spanish chicken with peppers 78
  Spanish lentils with couscous 80
  Penne Bolognaise 82
  Moroccan lamb with chilli, ginger 84
  Middle Eastern tagine 86
  Chilli con carne 88
  Balti curry 90
  Hake in green sauce 94
  Turkey braised in red wine 98
  Chicken rice 100
  Linguine carbonara 104
  Vegetarian mince 106
  Vegetable chilli 108
  Chicken with noodles 110
  Laksa 112
  Stuffed peppers 114
  Armenian lamb 116
  Pistachio pilaf 118
  Malaysian satay 120
  Satay sauce 122
Onions, spring 122
  Malaysian satay salad 122
Orange 32
  Fresh fruit salad
  Fennel and orange salad 70
Oregano, dried 13
  Penne Bolognaise 82
  Vegetable chilli 108
  Chicken with noodles 110
**P**
Parsley 58
  Hummus pitta bean tabbouleh 58
  Hake in green sauce 94
  Fish fillets with puy lentils 102

Pasta 12
  Penne Bolognaise 82
Peanut butter 122
  Satay sauce 122
Peas 12
Pepper, ground 22
  Spiced porridge 22
Peppers 60
  Huevos rancheros 60
  Roasted Mediterranean vegetable 74
  Spanish chicken with peppers 78
  Spanish lentils with couscous
  Penne Bolognaise 82
  Chilli con carne 88
  Chicken rice 100
  Vegetarian mince 106
  Vegetable chilli 108
  Stuffed peppers 114
Pesto 12
  Spinach and pesto quiche 56
  Fish fillets with puy lentils 102
Pies, fruit 12
Pineapple 122
  Malaysian satay salad 122
Pine nuts 44
  Spinach with raisins and pine nuts 44
  Stuffed peppers 114
Plums 138
  Fruit crumble 138
Pomegranate 68
  Quinoa salad 68
  Fennel and orange salad 70
Potatoes 13
  Spanish omelette 46
  Roasted Mediterranean vegetables 74
  Spanish chicken with peppers 78
  Balti curry 90
  Hake in green sauce 94
Provisioning 11
Prunes 12
  Fruit crumble 138
  Breton fruit cake 152
Pumpkin seeds 34
  Sunflower banana toast 34
  Dawn start oats 36
  Fruit crumble 138
**Q**
Quinoa 68

Quinoa salad 68
**R**
Radishes 66
  Mixed salad 66
Raisins 148
  Wheaty fruit load 148
Raspberries 32
  Fresh fruit salad 32
  Chocolate indulgence 144
Red wine sauce 84
  Moroccan lamb with chilli, ginger 84
  Middle Eastern tagine 86
Rice, wholemeal
  Chicken rice
  Stuffed peppers 114
Rosemary 74
  Roasted Mediterranean vegs 74
  Turkey in red wine 98
  Cheesy oat squares 158
Ryvita 12
  Sunflower banana toast 34
**S**
Salad vegetables 13
Salmon 100
  Fish fillets with puy lentils 102
Sandwich 48
Sausages, vegetarian 13
Seed mix 68
  Quinoa salad 68
  Sailor's trifle 140
  Wheaty fruit loaf 148
  Flapjack 156
  Cheesy oat squares 158
Sherry 140
  Sailor's trifle 140
Sesame seeds 138
  Fruit crumble 138
Shredded wheat 12
Smoked salmon 42
  Scrambled eggs with garlic and smoked salmon 42
Soup, tinned 12
Soy sauce 72
  Green vegetable stir fry 72
Spanish Chicken sauce 78
Spanish Omelette 46
Spinach 44
  Spinach with raisins and pine nuts 44
  Spinach and pesto quiche 56

Fish fillets with puy lentils 102
Chicken with noodles 110
Spring onions 42
  Scrambled eggs with garlic and smoked salmon 42
Mixed salad 66
Strawberries 32
  Fresh fruit salad 32
  Chocolate indulgence 144
Star anise 28
  Spiced dried fruit salad
Stock cubes 108
  Vegetable chilli 108
Stockpots 12
  Middle Eastern tagine 86
  Turkey in red wine 98
  Chicken rice 100
  Vegetarian mince 106
  Chicken with noodles 110
  Laksa 112
  Stuffed peppers 114
  Armenian lamb 116
  Pistachio pilaf 118
Sugar, brown 138
  Fruit crumble 138
  Wheaty fruit loaf 148
  Wholemeal bread 162
Sugar, molasses 150
  Beetroot and chocolate muffins 150
  Breton fruit cake 152
  Devon apple blueberry cake 154
  Flapjack 156
Sugar snap peas 90
  Balti curry 90
Sugar, white 12
  Penne Bolognaise 82
  Vegetarian mince 106
  Stuffed peppers 114
Sultanas 12
  Spiced porridge 22
Sunflower seeds 34
  Sunflower banana toast 34
  Dawn start oats 36
  Fruit crumble 138
Sweetcorn, baby fresh 90
  Balti curry 90
  Laksa 112
Sweetcorn, tinned 12
**T**
Tamarind paste 112
  Laksa 112

Satay sauce 122
Tapa 42
  Scrambled eggs with garlic and smoked salmon 42
Tea 12
Tea herbal 12
Textured soya protein chunks 12
  Middle Eastern tagine 86
Textured soya protein mince 12
  Vegetarian mince 106
Thyme 98
  Turkey braised in red wine 98
Tofu 13
Tomato, fresh 58
  Hummus pitta bean tabbouleh 58
  Chicken rice 100
  Tuna salad 64
  Mixed salad 66
  Quinoa salad 68
  Penne Bolognaise 82
  Balti curry 90
  Chicken with noodles 110
Tomato puree 12
  Penne Bolognaise 82
  Vegetarian mince 106
  Vegetable chilli 108
  Armenian lamb 116
Tomatoes, sundried 12
  Cheesy oat squares 158
Tomatoes, tinned chopped 12
  Huevos rancheros 60
  Spanish chicken with peppers 78
  Spanish lentils with couscous 80
  Moroccan lamb with chilli, ginger 84
  Middle Eastern tagine 86
  Chilli con carne 88
  Vegetarian mince 106
  Vegetable chilli 108
  Stuffed peppers 114
  Armenian lamb 116
Tortilla chips 88
Turkey 90
  Balti curry 90
  Turkey braised in red wine 98
Tuna, tinned 12
  Tuna salad 64
Turmeric, ground 13
  Spiced porridge 22
  Middle Eastern tagine 86
  Laksa 112
  Malaysian satay 120

**U**
**V**
Vanilla extract 150
  Beetroot and chocolate muffins 150
Vegetable bouillon 72
  Green vegetable stir fry 72
  Spanish lentils with couscous 80
  Penne Bolognaise 82
  Moroccan lamb with chilli, ginger 84
  Hake in green sauce 94
Vinegar 12
  Mushroom and kale eggs 30
  Tuna salad 64
  Mixed salad 66
  Fennel and orange salad 70
**W**
Watercress 68
  Quinoa salad 68
Water melon 68
  Quinoa salad 68
Walnuts 12
Wheat biscuits 148
Wheaty fruit loaf 148
Wholemeal flour, strong 12
  Wholemeal bread 162
Wholemeal rice 12
Wine, red 98
  Turkey braised in red wine
Wine, white 94
  Hake in green sauce 94
**X**
**Y**
Yeast, dried 12
  Wholemeal bread 162
Yogurt 13
  Dawn start oats
  Fish fillets with puy lentils
  Sailor's trifle 140
  Chocolate indulgence 144

**Z**

Under sail, heading south

# Recipe Index

| Recipe Title | Page |
|---|---|
| Apricot Almond Baked Custard | 142 |
| Armenian Lamb | 116 |
| Balti Curry | 90 |
| Bananajack | 154 |
| Bean Tabbouleh with Hummus | 58 |
| Beetroot and Chocolate Muffins | 150 |
| Cheesy Oat Squares | 158 |
| Breton Fruit Cake | 152 |
| Chicken Rice | 100 |
| Chicken with Noodles | 110 |
| Chilli con Carne | 88 |
| Chocolate Indulgence | 144 |
| Cooked Breakfast | 24 |
| Dawn Start Oats | 36 |
| Devon Apple Blueberry Cake | 154 |
| Fennel and Orange Salad | 70 |
| Fish Fillets with Puy Lentils | 102 |
| Fresh Fruit Salad | 32 |
| Fruit Crumble | 138 |
| Fruit Fool | 136 |
| Green Vegetable Stir-Fry | 72 |
| Gammon Steaks with Fried Eggs Mushrooms and Beans | 24 |
| Huevos Rancheros | 60 |
| Malaysian Satay Un-Skewered | 120 |
| Merluza en Salsa Verde | 94 |
| Middle Eastern Tagine | 86 |
| Mixed Salad | 66 |
| Moroccan Lamb with Chilli and Ginger | 84 |
| Mushroom and Kale Eggs | 30 |
| Laksa | 112 |
| Laying Up Cottage Pie | 128 |
| Laying Up Quiche | 132 |
| Leftovers Soup | 126 |
| Linguine Carbonara | 104 |

# Recipe Index

| Recipe Title | Page |
|---|---|
| Paella de Sobras | 130 |
| Penne Bolognaise | 82 |
| Pineapple Salad | 122 |
| Pistachio Pilaf | 118 |
| Poached Eggs on Toast | 26 |
| Quick Pastry Crust | 160 |
| Quinoa Salad | 68 |
| Red Coleslaw | 66 |
| Roasted Mediterranean Vegetables | 74 |
| Sandwiches | 48-55 |
| Satay Sauce | 122 |
| Scrambled Eggs with Garlic and Smoked Salmon | 42 |
| Seafarers Trifle | 140 |
| Spanish Chicken with Peppers | 78 |
| Spanish Lentils | 80 |
| Spanish Omelette | 46 |
| Spiced Dried Fruit Salad | 28 |
| Spiced Porridge | 22 |
| Spinach and Pesto Quiche | 56 |
| Spinach with Raisins and Pine Nuts | 44 |
| Stuffed Peppers Braised in Tomato Sauce | 114 |
| Turkey Braised in Red Wine | 98 |
| Sunflower Banana Toast | 34 |
| Tuna Salad | 64 |
| Vegetable Chilli | 108 |
| Vegetarian Mince | 106 |
| Wheaty Fruit Loaf | 148 |
| Wholemeal Bread | 162 |

## THE AUTHOR

Rosa Mari Edlin Williams is a Cordon Bleu cook who developed her passion for food as a young child 'helping' her Spanish mother and English father in the kitchen. This interest grew when cooking with her father at the weekends who instilled the pleasure of preparing diverse dishes and sharing them around the family dining table.

She has worked in Australia for the former Queensland Butter Marketing Board, demonstrated in High schools at the request of Home Economics teachers and at Australian Country Women's Association events showcasing their produce, devised and delivered evening classes and appeared on television promoting dairy produce. She assisted in preparing cookery pages as a food journalist in Sydney at Woman's Day with Margaret Fulton as editor and Suzanne Gibbs also a Cordon Bleu cook.

Living on board a trimaran on the Brisbane river in Queensland kindled a love of sailing which included sailing for two months from Singapore to Penang along the Malacca Straits. She has sailed in the Mediterranean in Greece, the Balearic islands and the south and east coast of Spain as well as Anglesey, Isle of Man, Northern Ireland, Scotland including the Crinan canal, the Isles of Scilly and Plymouth to La Rochelle.

Rosa is an FCCA with a Masters degree in forensic accounting but has always been passionate about well prepared, nutritious food in whatever environment it is cooked. She has two adult children and lives on Anglesey with her husband.

The author at the helm leaving the Scilly Isles, returning to Padstow

Sunset, in Victoria Dock, Caernarfon, North Wales

## Acknowledgments

I would like to acknowledge and thank all those RYA students who have tested some of these recipes for me while undertaking RYA courses together with my family, especially my husband, David, who has been asked to taste, constructively criticise, suggest additions, deletions and improvements as well as proofread the text several times. Needless to say there have been many cookery authors I have referred to for guidance and inspiration on book design and layout.

Early morning Tighnabruaich looking towards Loch Ruel

Printed in Great Britain
by Amazon